Pass the new
Life in
the UK
test

Celine Castelino
edited by Chris Taylor

niace

promoting adult learning

This text reproduces substantial content from the publication *Life in United Kingdom: A Guide for New Residents* (3rd edition), published by the Stationery Office (2013) on behalf of the Home Office. This information is licensed under the terms of the Open Government Licence (www.nationalarchives.gov.uk/doc/open-government-licence).

The material reproduced does not represent the views, opinions or policy of the National Institute of Adult Continuing Education (NIACE).

Published by the National Institute of Adult Continuing Education

NIACE (England and Wales)
21 De Montfort Street
Leicester LE1 7GE

Company registration no. 2603322

Charity registration no. 1002775

The National Institute of Adult Continuing Education (NIACE) is an independent charity which promotes adult learning across England and Wales. Through its research, development, publications, events, outreach and advocacy activity, NIACE works to improve the quality and breadth of opportunities available for all adults so they can benefit from learning throughout their lives.

www.niace.org.uk

For details of all our publications, visit http://shop.niace.org.uk

Follow NIACE on Twitter: @NIACEhq

@NIACEDC (Wales)

@NIACEbooks (Publications)

Cataloguing in Publications Data

A CIP record for this title is available from the British Library

978-1-86201-702-3 (print)
978-1-86201-703-0 (PDF)
978-1-86201-704-7 (ePub)
978-1-86201-705-4 (online)
978-1-86201-706-1 (Kindle)

All websites referenced in this book were correct and accessible at the time of going to press.

Printed in the UK by Page Bros (Norwich) Ltd

Designed and typeset by Book Production Services, London

Contents

Forewords v

Introduction 1

Chapter One How to use this book 3

Section 1 How the guide is organised 4

Section 2 How to study 7

Chapter Two Values and principles 18

Section 1 Values and principles 19

Section 2 Applying to become a permanent resident or citizen 22

Section 3 Taking the *Life in the UK* test 24

Section 4 What is the UK? 26

Chapter Three A long and illustrious history 32

Section 1 Early Britain 33

Section 2 The Middle Ages 44

Section 3 The Tudors and Stuarts 55

Section 4 A global power 80

Section 5 The 20th century 106

Section 6 Britain since 1945 115

Chapter Four A modern, thriving society 153

Section 1 The UK today 154

Section 2 Religion 162

Section 3 Customs and traditions 167

Section 4 Sport 174

Section 5 Arts and culture 182

Section 6 Leisure 196

Chapter Five The UK government, the law and your role   221

Section 1 The development of British democracy   222

Section 2 The British constitution   224

Section 3 The government   233

Section 4 Voting   244

Section 5 The UK and international institutions   249

Section 6 Respecting the law   253

Section 7 The role of the courts   259

Section 8 Fundamental principles   265

Section 9 Your role in the community   272

Chapter Six Taking the test   295

Section 1 Booking your test   296

Section 2 What to expect on the day of your test   301

Section 3 Tips to help you when you take the test   307

Section 4 What happens after the test?   309

Chapter Seven Practice tests   310

Chapter Eight Resources, references and useful websites   331

Forewords

'If I want to live in this country, I need to know about the history, government and day-to-day life here.' I have heard this kind of comment many times over the years from ESOL (English for Speakers of Other Languages) learners attending 'ESOL with citizenship' classes; they have made a commitment to the UK and thus have a real need and desire to learn about the country they now regard as home.

For most migrants, learning English and adapting to a new way of life in a new country present many challenges. Making the decision to apply for citizenship is a big step and the requirement for all applicants to take the *Life in the UK test* is yet another hurdle for applicants to overcome.

Preparing for the *Life in the UK* test involves reading and understanding the official material in *Life in the UK: A Guide for New Residents,* (3rd edition) – a daunting task, especially for those who may not have a high level of literacy in English. Consequently, a self-study guide written in 'plain English' is a very welcome development.

This readable study guide is written in a clear, systematic and structured way. It not only supports readers in developing their understanding of the potentially difficult material in the official guide but also, by focusing on 'active learning' and study skills, provides essential help in learning key information and facts, especially for those who may not have studied for a long time.

I believe that this complete study guide will prove invaluable as excellent preparation and practice material for anyone intending to take the *Life in the UK* test.

Judith Kirsh
Co-chair of NATECLA, the National Association for Teaching English and other Community Languages to Adults

NIACE is committed to ensuring all learners get the best chance to succeed. That is why we have published this book to support those people who want to take the *Life in the UK* test.

Celine Castelino has written a clear and helpful guide designed particularly for those people whose second language is English. As an ESOL specialist, Celine worked for many years for the Basic Skills Agency. Recognised for her expertise, she was invited by Sir Bernard Crick to join the Advisory Board on Naturalisation and Integration (ABNI) and was closely involved in the development of the test.

She has given us easy steps to learning, checks and mini-tests, activities and suggestions to make learning the new *Life in the United Kingdom* handbook that much easier. As the editor, I was pleased to work alongside Celine to produce this guide. Between us, we have more than fifty years of teaching and management experience in ESOL. We hope this helps you to pass the test – good luck!

Chris Taylor
NIACE Programme Manager for ESOL

Introduction

You have come a long way on your journey to becoming a UK citizen. Your next step is to take the *Life in the UK* test. It may be a long time since you studied for a test, or took one. Are you nervous? Don't be. Our self-study guide has all the information you need to prepare and practise for the test.

We have included all of the official study material you need to know to pass the test from *Life in the United Kingdom: A Guide for New Residents* (3rd Edition). We have explained the parts that are difficult and added lots of tips and techniques to make learning easier. There are questions at the end of each chapter for you to check how much you remember. At the end of the book you will find sample tests written in the same style as the official test so you can practise and become familiar with them.

The government decided to introduce the *Life in the UK* test in 2005 to encourage people applying to live here permanently to learn more about UK society: its rich culture, traditions, structures and ways of life. The first handbook and test were revised in 2007 and once again in 2013. There have also been changes to the process for becoming a citizen or gaining the right to settle in the UK.

Applicants for citizenship or settlement must now have an English speaking and listening qualification at Level B1 (ESOL Entry 3) or above. We have written the study guide in plain English so that it is as easy to read as possible by people from different language backgrounds. The writer and editor are specialists in the fields of citizenship and English for Speakers of Other Languages.

The questions in the test only cover the information in *Life in the United Kingdom: A Guide for New Residents* (3rd Edition). They are not meant to catch you out but to make sure that you have read and remembered the facts and other information in the book. Our questions are similar and are intended to help you prepare for the test.

Working your way through this book and completing the tasks in it will give you the best chance of passing the test first time.

CHAPTER ONE

How to use this book

This chapter tells you what information is in this study guide and how best to use it. It explains who needs to take the test and how to apply for it. It is divided into the following two sections:

- **Section 1** How the guide is organised
- **Section 2** Study tips

■ SECTION 1 How the guide is organised

Most people find it easiest to learn a little at a time. We have broken up the study material from the handbook *Life in the United Kingdom: A Guide for New Residents* (3rd Edition) into short sections and used diagrams, summaries and brief explanations to help you understand different topics. You can use the questions called **Check your learning** to check how you are progressing. Our **Study tips** section has different techniques on how to study more effectively. There are additional **Study tips** throughout the book. People learn in many different ways, so try them out and use the ones that work best for you.

You must read all the study material from the handbook. It contains the information you need to know for the test. Make sure you know it well. We have included all the study material you need in Chapters Two to Five.

There is a **glossary** at the end of each chapter. This provides a simple definition or explanation of words and phrases from the study material that might be difficult to understand. Words and phrases that are underlined in the text are listed in the glossary.

Chapter Six tells you about taking the test and what should happen on the day of your test.

There are four practice tests at the end of the book (Chapter Seven). They are written in the same format (style) as the *Life in the UK* test. There are 24 multiple-choice questions in each one, as in the official test.

ⓘ NOTE

Some of the facts and figures in the study material might be different from what you know or read elsewhere. The test questions only ask about the information in the study material from *Life in the United Kingdom: A Guide for New Residents* (3rd Edition). You won't be asked about changes in the law or regulations, or other facts not mentioned in this study guide.

How each chapter about the study materials is organised

All the chapters on the study material follow the same layout. They include:

- a brief introduction with a list of the main points from the chapter;
- the study material from *Life in the UK: A Guide for New Residents* (3rd Edition), including questions and tasks to check you understand what you have read;
- revision questions to help reinforce your learning and find out if you have missed or forgotten anything, and an end-of-chapter checklist to remind you what you have learnt; and
- answers to the tasks in the chapter.

The study material

We have printed the study material from the *Life in the UK* guide in short sections like the one below. The beginning and end of the sections are marked with a Union Jack flag, as in the following example:

🇬🇧 The Norman Conquest

In 1066, an invasion led by William, the Duke of Normandy (in what is now northern France), defeated Harold, the Saxon king of England, at the Battle of Hastings. Harold was killed in the battle. William became king of England and is known as William the Conqueror. The battle is commemorated in a great piece of embroidery, known as the Bayeux Tapestry, which can still be seen in France today. 🇬🇧

i NOTE

The test is made up of multiple-choice questions. You don't have to write anything. You don't have to know how to spell or pronounce any of the words from the study material, you just need to be able to understand them.

Features used in the guide

1. Check your learning

There are questions after each short section of the study material. Use them to check what you have learnt and how much you remember. If you are not sure of the answers, read the material again or turn to the end of the chapter where you will find the answers. Take a break, then try to answer the questions again.

2. Study tips

We have included ideas, tips and techniques to help you learn, remember and prepare for the day of your test. In addition to the general advice in this chapter, there are tips to help you learn particular information throughout the book.

3. Note

This feature reminds you of important information. For example, a note beside a list of famous people will remind you that you do not have to remember their dates of birth or death; it is enough to know the century or period when they were important.

4. Find out more

These are interesting facts on each topic. There are no questions on the information in the **Find out more** boxes, so you do not have to learn it.

■ SECTION 2 How to study

This section has advice and study tips to help you remember what you have learnt quickly and effectively. People learn in many different ways. Some like to read over and over again, while others take notes, draw pictures, record and listen to the information, or write down questions to ask themselves later. Active learning works best for most people. This means doing more than just reading the study material and repeating it. By active learning we mean using your senses – sight, touch, hearing or speaking – as well as your memory and your imagination. The guidance that follows suggests different methods for active learning. Choose the ones that work best for you.

Planning your study time

Planning time when you will study is one of the best things you can do. Little and often works best for most people. Make a timetable like the one on the next page and give yourself plenty of time before your test date. If you stick to it, you will feel more confident and less stressed than if you leave your studying to the last minute.

Organise your study time into short periods and take lots of breaks. If you are not used to studying, start with 10–15 minutes and gradually increase the time. Pay attention to how you feel. When you begin to find it hard to concentrate – stop. Get up and move, do something completely different: stretch, take a walk, have something to eat or drink, put on your favourite music, call a friend or whatever works for you. Return to your studying when you feel more refreshed.

Try studying at different times of the day to find what time suits you best. Many employers are willing to give employees time off to study during work hours so if you are in a job, do ask. Some people wake up earlier in the morning to study, others prefer to learn in the evening or even late at night. Just make sure you get enough sleep. It is difficult to concentrate when you are tired.

Time	Morning	Lunch break/afternoon	Evening
Monday	Read pages 30–35 before work	Tell study buddy what I've learnt, ask each other questions	30/40 minutes Read 5–10 pages, write questions on cards Have a break Write brief notes about topic
Tuesday	Read next 5–10 pages on train/bus	Talk to friend at work about politics	Watch a history programme on television Read study materials about that topic
Wednesday	Read my notes on chapter before work	Arrange to visit council/Assembly/Parliament	Watch *Today in Parliament* for 15 minutes Start next chapter 30–40 minutes
Thursday	Read / listen to notes	Meet study buddy	Go to exercise class Do revision questions from Chapter 3 Reread study material
Friday	Start work early	—	Leave work early and visit museum on the way home
Saturday	Visit a monument/museum/gallery	Study/take notes/draw a spider diagram	Relax, go out, see friends
Sunday	—	—	Revise Start next section Plan for next week

Some people like to study with music playing in the background; others need peace and quiet. If you need a quiet place and there is nowhere at home or work, try a public library or community centre. When the weather is good, you could take your books to a park or other open space.

Do you know someone else studying for the test? Why not ask them to be your study buddy and help each other to learn? You could each learn a different topic and then teach it to your buddy or buddies. Discuss it and then use the **Check your learning** questions to make sure each of you has understood the topic.

You can write down your own questions about each topic as you read them. Give them to your study buddy or a friend to ask you. You could write down answers separately or just check them in the study material.

Study tip

Did you know that talking about what you have learnt or explaining it to someone else can help you to remember and understand the information better?

How do you remember what you read or learn? Do you learn best by reading and taking notes, by drawing pictures or diagrams, or by listening to information and repeating it aloud? Use whatever method is most helpful to you.

Make sure you have everything you need to study – for example, paper or a notebook, pens and pencils, highlighters and a dictionary. If you can record your voice on your mobile phone, use it to record your notes so you can listen to them later.

Where do you start?

Read to remember

You will have to read and remember a lot of detailed information. Good ways to do this are as follows:

- Look at the title of each section and think about what you already know about the topic.
- Notice how the section is organised. There are:
  - headings in **bold** to tell you what is in the passage below;
  - lists with bullet points like this one at the start of each chapter; and
  - key passages marked with a Union Jack.

We use these features to make it easier for you to read and identify what is important to know.

- Look at other features: pictures, diagrams, tables or maps.

- Get a feel for the section – read it quickly and ask yourself these questions:
  - What are the key points?
  - What do I remember?

- Read the section again slowly and in detail. Read it more than once if it helps. Next:
  - write the key points in your own words;
  - check your notes against the section;
  - correct your notes if necessary; and
  - add any important points you missed.

Put aside your notes and cover the section you have just read. Answer the questions in the **Check your learning** box at the end of the section without looking at your notes.

Plan a review every few days or once a week. Before you learn anything new, read your notes again then go back to the questions at the end of each section and answer them.

 Study tip

Research shows that we quickly forget about 80% of what we read. Doing something active, such as taking notes, highlighting key points or talking about the topic soon after you read it, helps you remember more of the information.

Making notes

Notes written in your own words, in English or, if you like, in your own language:

■ help you to remember what you have read;

■ are useful for revision; and

■ are shorter and quicker to read and learn.

You could write your notes in this guide or in a notebook or on cards.
   Reasons to make notes directly in this guide include:

■ it is quick and easy to write in the <u>margins</u>;

■ you only have one book to think about; and

■ you can use a <u>highlighter</u> pen or underline to mark key points.

Reasons to write notes separately from the guide could be that:

■ you have <u>summarised</u> what you have read in your own words to help you understand and remember; and

■ you will have short notes to revise, so you do not have to read the whole guide again.

You could do both if you wish.
   There are different ways to make and organise your notes, as follows:

■ Write the main points from each section on pieces of paper or cards.

■ Do not write too much detail. Have one key piece of information on each card with spaces between sentences so they are easy to read and remember.

■ Write your own questions on your cards. You can use them to test yourself or give them to someone else to test you.

■ Some people find that using different coloured pens or pencils to highlight important information – names, dates, numbers, etc. – helps them to remember facts more easily.

If you can, put the cards in places where you will see them frequently – for example, on a pin board, a mirror or your fridge.

Study tip

Did you know that your brain continues to think about what you are studying while you are asleep or during study breaks? Do not worry if you cannot remember information or facts immediately – your brain may still be working on the information.

Checking your understanding

When you have finished reading a section, put your book down. Ask yourself what the main points are and describe them in your own words. If you have a study buddy, explain the topic to him or her. If you are studying alone it still helps to do this aloud if you can – pretend you are teaching someone else. Some people find it helpful to record what they learn on their phone, computer or voice recorder.

Use your imagination and creativity to help you remember. You can also try the techniques listed below to help you remember what you need to know.

Mnemonics

A mnemonic (pronounced *nem-onic*) is a memory aid; a technique for helping your brain to remember something. Mnemonics are commonly used for remembering lists, spellings, numbers or learning a new language. The word comes from Ancient Greek and means 'of memory'. Mnemonics do not need to make sense. A common mnemonic is to use the first letter of each word you need to remember and use them to make up a sentence or story. Humour helps to make a mnemonic more memorable. For example, the sentence below:

No **P**lan **L**ike **Y**ours **T**o **S**tudy **H**istory **W**isely

could help you remember the British royal families in the right order:

Normandy, Plantagenet, Lancaster, York, Tudor, Stuart, Hanover, Windsor

Or you could use more than one letter at the start of the word. This sentence reminds you of the names of the four UK capital cities:

Ed Loves **Car Bel**ls
Edinburgh, **Lo**ndon, **Car**diff, **Bel**fast

The best mnemonics are ones that make you laugh or that you make up when you are learning. This helps make strong connections in your brain.

You can also use pictures in your mind to help you fix the information in your memory. So to remember Ed Loves Car Bells, you could imagine a man dressed in a tartan kilt with Ed written on his shirt or his cap, looking lovingly at a car covered in bells. You could add details – the word 'love' could be made out of London sights, the car could look like a Welsh dragon, and the bells could be in the shape of flax flowers from the Northern Ireland Assembly logo. Yes, it is silly, but you will remember it.

Spider diagrams

If you find it easier to remember what you see, you are a visual learner. Spider diagrams or mind maps should work for you. Use them to link facts together. Colours and pictures will make them even more memorable. The spider diagram on the next page contains key information on the four parts of the UK.

Diagrams

Drawings, pictures and diagrams are a wonderful way of recording and organising information. If you create the diagram yourself it will be more meaningful to you and therefore easier to recall the important facts you record.

You could make diagrams or drawings on sheets of paper or cards. Place or pin them somewhere you will see them frequently until you remember what is on them.

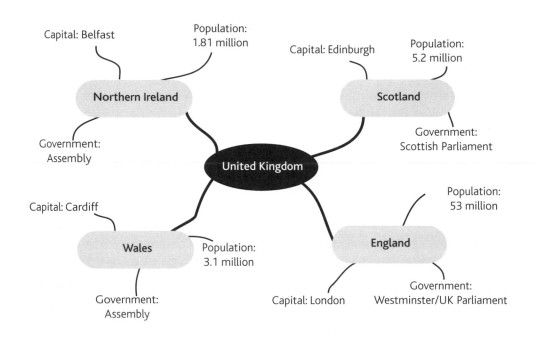

Figure 1: Spider diagram to show key information about the four parts of the UK.

Remembering dates

Many people find dates and numbers that mean little to them difficult to remember. If this is you, try some of the following tips:

■ Make up a rhyme about the date. A well-known example from America is:

In fourteen hundred and ninety-two, Columbus sailed the ocean blue.

to remember the date **1492** when Christopher Columbus discovered America.

■ If you enjoy singing, repeat the dates – or your rhyme – to a musical beat.

■ Create a sentence in which the number of letters in each word are the same as the number you want to remember, e.g. for Columbus: A (**1**) good (**4**) discovery (**9**) is (**2**). If you find it easier, use words from your home language.

- Make the date memorable by linking it to personal information – the year you, or a family member or friend, were born; or the number of a house where you lived.

- Link a date or number to information from the country where you were born. So to remember that British women over the age of 21 got the right to vote in 1928, link it to the date when women could vote in that country or an event you know about that happened during that year.

- Try imagining the numbers as pictures or shapes. Number 1 could be a post or stick, 2 a swan, 3 a fork, etc; or 3 is a triangle and 4 a square and so on.

Difficult words

Using a dictionary to look up every word you do not understand will slow you down and could make you feel frustrated. Try to work out the meaning of the word using the information from the rest of the sentence or paragraph. Ask yourself if it is important to know what a word means to understand the sentence or idea – you do not always need to know the meaning of every word to understand a sentence.

If there are lots of words you do not understand, write them down and continue reading. When you have finished reading a passage or section, look them up, write down what they mean in your notes or in a small notebook, then read the passage again.

Don't forget that you can look up many of the words in the glossaries at the end of each chapter of this book, which tell you what words and phrases in the study materials mean.

If you have access to the internet, you could use Google Translate. However, use it with care as it is not always accurate!

Revision

Include time for revision in your study plan. Reviewing what you learnt a week or two before your test will help to store the information more firmly in your memory. You will be surprised how much you remember – this will help your confidence. Use the revision questions at the end of each chapter, together with the tasks in the chapters.

Ask a friend, relative or study buddy to help you by asking you questions from this study guide or by making up questions using your notes or the cards you have made. You could explain some of the things you have learnt to someone else. They might enjoy learning something new.

i NOTE

The questions in this book are not taken from the test. We wrote them to help you to check what you have learnt and to decide when you are ready to take the test. The test questions will be different from ours.

Glossary

creativity	Using your imagination to produce new or unusual ideas, pictures or things.
highlight	Make something stand out – highlighter pens apply colour.
imagination	The part of your mind that creates ideas, pictures or feelings that are not real.
logo	A design or symbol used to represent a place, organisation or company.
margins	The white space on a page between the main content and the edge.

summarised Shorten a long text to include only the most important points about a topic.

techniques Methods or special ways of doing something.

CHAPTER TWO

Values and principles

In this chapter you will read the official study material and learn about the values and principles that good citizens share and respect. You will also learn about the process of becoming a permanent resident or citizen of the UK.

To help you learn the information, we have divided the chapter into the following sections:

- **Section 1** Values and principles
- **Section 2** Applying to become a permanent resident or citizen
- **Section 3** Taking the *Life in the UK* test
- **Section 4** What is the UK?

i NOTE

You need to read all the official study material carefully. The test questions can ask you about any of the study material in every chapter, including this one.

You may find some of the words difficult. Most of them are explained in the glossary at the end of the chapter. It is a good idea to use a dictionary to check and make a note of any other key words you do not understand.

SECTION 1 Values and principles

In this section you will read about:

- **the values and principles of the UK**
- **the citizenship ceremony**
- **the responsibilities and freedoms enjoyed by all who live in the UK**

Study tip

Read each section once quickly to get an idea of what it is about.
Read it again more slowly. Pay special attention to any features such as words in **bold** and bullet points.
Ask yourself: What did I know already? What new information am I learning? What do I not understand?
Look up words you do not understand in the glossary or in a dictionary.

The values and principles of the UK

Britain is a fantastic place to live: a modern, thriving society with a long and illustrious history. Our people have been at the heart of the world's political, scientific, industrial and cultural development. We are proud of our record of welcoming new migrants who will add to the diversity and dynamism of our national life.

Applying to become a permanent resident or citizen of the UK is an important decision and commitment. You will be agreeing to accept the responsibilities which go with permanent residence and to respect the laws, values and traditions of the UK. Good citizens are an asset to the UK. We welcome those seeking to make a positive contribution to our society.

Passing the *Life in the UK* test is part of demonstrating that you are ready to become a permanent migrant to the UK. This handbook is designed to support you in your preparation. It will help you to integrate into society and play a full role in your local community. It will also help ensure that you have a broad general knowledge of the culture, laws and history of the UK.

British society is founded on fundamental values and principles which all those living in the UK should respect and support. These values are reflected in the responsibilities, rights and privileges of being a British citizen or permanent resident of the UK. They are based on history and traditions and are protected by law, customs and expectations. There is no place in British society for extremism or intolerance.

The fundamental principles of British life include:

■ democracy
■ the rule of law
■ individual liberty
■ tolerance of those with different faiths and beliefs
■ participation in community life.

As part of the citizenship ceremony, new citizens pledge to uphold these values. The pledge is:

'I will give my loyalty to the United Kingdom and respect its rights and freedoms. I will uphold its democratic values. I will observe its laws faithfully and fulfil my duties and obligations as a British citizen.'

Flowing from the fundamental principles are **responsibilities and freedoms** which are shared by all those living in the UK and which we expect all residents to respect.

If you wish to be a permanent resident or citizen of the UK, you should:

■ respect and obey the law
■ respect the rights of others, including their right to their own opinions

- treat others with fairness
- look after yourself and your family
- look after the area in which you live and the environment.

In return, the UK offers:

- freedom of belief and religion
- freedom of speech
- freedom from <u>unfair discrimination</u>
- a right to a fair trial
- a right to join in the election of a government.

Check your learning

2.1 Tolerance of those with other faiths and participation in community life are two of the principles that British citizens support. Can you name another two principles?

1._____ 2._____

2.2 Is the following statement **True** or **False**?

It is against the law in the UK to say you do not agree with the government in public.

Did you know?

Before the law protected the right to free speech, people who disagreed with the government could talk about their opinions at a place called Speakers' Corner in Hyde Park, in London. Many other cities in the UK and Europe have similar places where people make speeches about different subjects. By tradition, they can say whatever they like as long as it is not offensive or against the law.

■ SECTION 2 Applying to become a permanent resident or citizen

In this section you will read about:

■ **what you have to do to apply to become a permanent resident or citizen before October 2013**

■ **what you need to do after October 2013**

> **Did you know?**
>
> Over 150,000 people took the *Life in the UK* test in 2012.

▓ Becoming a permanent resident

To apply to become a permanent resident or citizen of the UK, you will need to:

■ speak and read English

■ have a good understanding of life in the UK.

There are currently (as of January 2013) two ways you can be tested on these requirements:

■ Take the *Life in the UK* test. The questions are written in a way that requires an understanding of the English language at English for Speakers of Other Languages (ESOL) Entry Level 3, so there is no need to take a separate English language test. People here on work visas, including those on Tier 1 and Tier 2 of the points-based system, normally must pass the *Life in the UK* test to become permanent residents.

■ Pass an ESOL course in English with Citizenship. You will need to take this course if your standard of English is below ESOL Entry Level 3. The course will help you to improve your English and learn more about life in the UK. At the end of the course you will take a test.

Once you have passed one of these tests, you can make an application for permanent residence or British citizenship. The form that you have to complete and the evidence that you need to provide will depend on your personal circumstances. There is a fee for submitting an application, which is different for the various types of application. All of the forms and a list of fees can be found on the UK Border Agency website, www.ukba.homeoffice.gov.uk

From October 2013, the requirements will change. From that date, for settlement or permanent residence you will need to:

■ Pass the *Life in the UK* test **AND**

■ Produce acceptable evidence of speaking and listening skills in English at B1 of the Common European Framework of Reference. This is equivalent to ESOL Entry Level 3.

The requirements for citizenship applications may also change in the future. Further details will be published on the UK Border Agency website and you should check the information on that website for current requirements before applying for settlement or citizenship.

Check your learning

2.3 Without looking at the text, write down two groups of people who have to take the *Life in the UK* test.

1. _____ 2._____

■ SECTION 3 Taking the *Life in the UK* test

In this section you will read about:

- ■ the *Life in the UK* test
- ■ where to find further information

■ Taking the *Life in the UK* test

This book will help prepare you for taking the *Life in the UK* test. The test consists of 24 questions about important aspects of life in the UK. Questions are based on ALL parts of the marked study material. The 24 questions will be different for each person taking the test at that test session.

The *Life in the UK* test is usually taken in English, although special arrangements can be made if you wish to take it in Welsh or Scottish Gaelic.

You can only take the test at a registered and approved *Life in the UK* test centre. There are about 60 test centres around the UK. You can only book your test online, at www.lifeintheuktest.gov.uk. You should not take your test at any other establishment as the UK Border Agency will only accept certificates from registered test centres.

If you live on the Isle of Man or in the Channel Islands, there are different arrangements for taking the *Life in the UK* test.

When booking your test, read the instructions carefully. Make sure you enter your details correctly. You will need to take some identification and proof of your address with you to the test. If you don't take these, you will not be able to take the test. ■

How to use this guide

Everything that you will need to know to pass the *Life in the UK* test is included in the study material in this book. The questions will be based on the whole book, including this chapter, so make sure you study the entire book thoroughly. This guide has been written to ensure that anyone who can read English at ESOL Entry Level 3 or above should have no difficulty with the language.

The glossaries at the end of each chapter contain some key words and phrases, which you might find helpful.

The **Check your understanding** sections are for guidance. They will help you to identify particular things that you should understand. Just knowing the things <u>highlighted</u> in these sections will not be enough to pass the test. You need to make sure that you understand everything in the book, so please read the information carefully.

Where to find more information

You can find out more information from the following places:

- The UK Border Agency website (www.ukba.homeoffice.gov.uk) for more information about the application process and the forms you will need to complete

- The *Life in the UK* test website (www.lifeintheuktest.gov.uk) for more information about the test and how to book a place to take one

- Gov.uk (www.gov.uk) for information about ESOL courses and how to find one in your area.

Check your learning

2.4 How many questions are there in the *Life in the UK* test? Tick the box next to the correct answer:

☐ 14
☐ 24
☐ 34
☐ 44

2.5 Name two things you must take with you to the test centre to be allowed to take the test.

1._____ 2. _____

i NOTE

This book contains **all** the text from the Home Office book, *Life in the UK: A Guide for New Residents* (3rd Edition), plus study tips, questions and answers to help you pass the *Life in the UK* test. We have made some changes to help you, as follows:

- Glossaries at the end of each chapter explain difficult words. These definitions explain what the words mean in the sentence in which they are used. There are more words in our glossaries than in the original book.

■ SECTION 4 What is the UK?

In this section you will read about the different parts of the United Kingdom or UK.

⊞ What is the UK?

The UK is made up of England, Scotland, Wales and Northern Ireland. The rest of Ireland is an independent country.

The official name of the country is the United Kingdom of Great Britain and Northern Ireland. 'Great Britain' refers only to England, Scotland and Wales, not to Northern Ireland. The words 'Britain', 'British Isles' or 'British', however, are used in this book to refer to everyone in the UK.

There are also several islands which are closely linked with the UK but are not part of it: the Channel Islands and the Isle of Man. These have their own governments and are called 'Crown dependencies'. There are also several British overseas territories in other parts of the world, such as St Helena and the Falkland Islands. They are also linked to the UK but are not a part of it.

The UK is governed by the parliament sitting in Westminster. Scotland, Wales and Northern Ireland also have parliaments or assemblies of their own, with devolved powers in defined areas. ⊞

Check your learning

2.6 Tick the box next to the place that **is** part of the United Kingdom:

- ☐ The Isle of Man
- ☐ Wales
- ☐ St Helena
- ☐ The Falkland Islands

Did you know?

St Helena, a small island in the middle of the Atlantic Ocean, is Britain's second oldest remaining colony (now called an overseas territory). It was once the prison of the French Emperor Napoleon I from 1815 and, about 70 years later, of Dinuzulu kaCetshwayo, King of the Zulus in South Africa.

Check your understanding

Now that you have read Chapter Two, what can you remember about the following?

- ▪ the fundamental principles that British society believes in
- ▪ the values that come from the principles shared by British people
- ▪ the responsibilities and freedoms that come with permanent residence
- ▪ the process of becoming a permanent resident or citizen
- ▪ the different countries that make up the UK
- ▪ what the Crown dependencies and overseas territories are

Revision questions and end of chapter checklist

You have completed Chapter Two. Now that you have read the study materials, checked your learning and done a few tasks, try to answer the following revision questions. If you are not sure of the answers, use your notes or look back at the study material before checking the answers at the end of this chapter.

Revision questions

1 Everyone living in the UK should respect and support its fundamental values and what else?

Answer:

2 Are you allowed to follow your own religion in the UK?

Answer:

3 From October 2013, you have to produce a certificate to show you have passed an English Speaking and Listening test, and what else?

Answer:

4 The UK is made up of Scotland, Wales, Northern Ireland and which other country?

Answer:

5 Are the Channel Islands part of the UK?

Answer:

End of Chapter Two checklist

Now that you have come to the end of Chapter Two, tick the boxes when you have:

- read the study material ☐
- made short notes to help you with your revision ☐
- looked up words that you do not understand and made a note of them ☐
- completed the 'Check your learning' and revision questions and checked your answers ☐
- read the study material again for any questions you got wrong ☐

Glossary

asset	A person, skill or quality which is useful or helps you to succeed.
Crown dependency	A type of state with its own government and the Queen as head of state.
democracy	(here) A nation that believes in the right to elect its government.
devolved	Pass power from one group to another.
dynamism	Constant change or movement.
establishment	(here) Organisation.
expectations	Good things you expect to happen in the future.
fundamental	Most important or main part of something.
highlighted	Made to stand out, given more importance.
illustrious	Famous, admired and respected for achievements.
obligations	Duties; things you have to do.
pledge	A serious promise.
principles	Rules or beliefs about what is right and wrong that guide how people behave.
privileges	Benefits or advantages; the chance do something special.
registered test centres	Official centres accepted by the government.
tolerance	Allowing people to do or believe what they want, even if you do not agree.
traditions	A way of behaving or a belief that has continued for a long time among a group of people.
unfair discrimination	Treating a person or people in a worse way because they are different from you.
uphold	To support a decision, principle or law.
values	Beliefs about what is morally right and wrong and what is most important in society.

Answers to 'Check your learning' questions

2.1 Democracy, the rule of law, or individual liberty

2.2 False

2.3 People applying for permanent residence and people applying to become citizens

2.4 24

2.5 1. Identification 2. Proof of address

2.6 Wales

Answers to revision questions

1   Principles
2   Yes
3   Pass the *Life in the UK* test
4   England
5   No

CHAPTER THREE

A long and illustrious history

In this chapter you will read the official study material about the UK's history. It describes how our nation developed and changed. You will learn about monuments, famous people, battles and inventions that have changed our lives. This chapter has a lot of information and is divided into the following six sections:

Section 1 Early Britain

Section 2 The Middle Ages

Section 3 The Tudors and Stuarts

Section 4 A global power

Section 5 The 20th century

Section 6 Britain since 1945

i NOTE

You may read history books, or articles in newspapers, which do not agree with the information in these chapters. To pass the test it is important that you learn the information in the study material sections. You do **not** need to remember dates of birth or death for the test.

■ SECTION 1 Early Britain

In this section you will read about:

■ **Early Britain**

■ **the Romans**

■ **the Anglo-Saxons**

■ **the Vikings**

■ **the Norman Conquest**

■ Early Britain

The first people to live in Britain were <u>hunter-gatherers</u>, in what we call the Stone Age. For much of the Stone Age, Britain was connected to the continent by a land bridge. People came and went, following the herds of deer and horses which they hunted. Britain only became permanently separated from the continent by the Channel about 10,000 years ago.

The first farmers arrived in Britain 6,000 years ago. The <u>ancestors</u> of these first farmers probably came from south-east Europe. These people built houses, <u>tombs</u> and <u>monuments</u> on the land. One of these monuments, Stonehenge, still stands in what is now the English county of Wiltshire. Stonehenge was probably a special gathering place for seasonal ceremonies. Other Stone Age sites have also survived. Skara Brae on Orkney, off the north coast of Scotland, is the best <u>preserved</u> prehistoric village in northern Europe, and has helped archaeologists to understand more about how people lived near the end of the Stone Age.

Around 4,000 years ago, people learned to make bronze. We call this period the Bronze Age. People lived in roundhouses and buried their dead in tombs called round barrows. The people of the Bronze Age were <u>accomplished</u> metalworkers who made many beautiful objects in bronze and gold, including tools, ornaments and weapons. The Bronze Age was followed by the Iron Age, when people learned how to make weapons and tools out of iron. People still lived in roundhouses, grouped together into larger settlements, and sometimes defended sites called hill forts. A very impressive hill fort can still be seen today at Maiden Castle, in the English county of Dorset. Most people were farmers, craft workers or warriors. The language they spoke was part of the Celtic language family. Similar languages were spoken across Europe in the Iron Age, and related languages are still spoken today in some parts of Wales, Scotland and Ireland. The people of the Iron Age had a <u>sophisticated</u> culture and economy. They made the first coins to be <u>minted</u> in Britain, some inscribed with the names of Iron Age kings. This marks the beginnings of British history.

Find out more

Skara Brae is older than Stonehenge. It has been called the 'Scottish Pompeii' because so much of the buildings remain.

Check your learning

3.1 Read the study material carefully, then cover it and complete these sentences:

A. Britain was separated from the continent of Europe about _____ years ago.

B. People started farming in Britain about _____ years ago.

3.2 Is the following statement **True** or **False**?

Languages spoken in Wales, Scotland and Ireland belong to the Celtic language family.

3.3 The table on the next page has key information about the monuments from the text on Early Britain. Find the missing information from the text above and put it in the right boxes. We have started it for you:

What is the monument?	© Jule Berlin / Shutterstock.com	© Pecold / Shutterstock.com	© Major George Allen / Ashmolean
	Skara Brae	Stonehenge	Maiden Castle
Where is it?	Orkney, Scotland	Wiltshire, England	
When was it built?	Stone Age		Iron Age

🏴 The Romans

Julius Caesar led a Roman invasion of Britain in 55 BC. This was unsuccessful and for nearly 100 years Britain remained separate from the Roman Empire. In AD 43 the Emperor Claudius led the Roman army in a new invasion. This time, there was resistance from some of the British tribes but the Romans were successful in occupying almost all of Britain. One of the tribal leaders who fought against the Romans was Boudicca, the queen of the Iceni in what is now eastern England. She is still remembered today and there is a statue of her on Westminster Bridge in London, near the Houses of Parliament.

Areas of what is now Scotland were never conquered by the Romans, and the Emperor Hadrian built a wall in the north of England to keep out the Picts (ancestors of the Scottish people). Included in the wall were a number of forts. Parts of Hadrian's Wall, including the forts of Housesteads and Vindolanda, can still be seen. It is a popular area for walkers and is a UNESCO (United Nations Educational, Scientific and Cultural Organization) World Heritage Site.

The Romans remained in Britain for 400 years. They built roads and public buildings, created a structure of law, and introduced new plants and animals. It was during the 3rd and 4th centuries AD that the first Christian communities began to appear in Britain. 🏴

Statue of Boudicca on Westminster Bridge, London

Find out more

The Romans brought many new foods to Britain – including apples, carrots, celery, leeks, pears and turnips – as well as herbs and spices such as bay leaves, garlic, parsley, rosemary and thyme.

Roman citizens who came to Britain were of different races and from countries in Africa, Europe and the Middle East. They imported food from their countries and may even have opened the first kebab shops in the UK!

Check your learning

3.4 Which of these statements is correct?

☐   Julius Caesar invaded and ruled Britain in 55 BC.

☐   Julius Caesar tried to invade Britain in 55 BC but failed.

🏴 The Anglo-Saxons

The Roman army left Britain in AD 410 to defend other parts of the Roman Empire and never returned. Britain was again <u>invaded</u> by tribes from northern Europe: the Jutes, the Angles and the Saxons. The languages they spoke are the basis of modern-day English. Battles were fought against these invaders but, by about AD 600, Anglo-Saxon kingdoms were established in Britain. These kingdoms were mainly in what is now England. The burial place of one of the kings was at Sutton Hoo in modern Suffolk. This king was buried with treasure and armour, all placed in a ship which was then covered by a mound of earth. Parts of the west of Britain, including much of what is now Wales, and Scotland, remained free of Anglo-Saxon rule.

The Anglo-Saxons were not Christians when they first came to Britain but, during this period, <u>missionaries</u> came to Britain to preach about Christianity. Missionaries from Ireland spread the religion in the north. The most famous of these were St Patrick, who would become the <u>patron saint</u> of Ireland (see pages 165–166 for more about patron saints), and St Columba, who <u>founded</u> a <u>monastery</u> on the island of Iona, off the coast of what is now Scotland. St Augustine led missionaries from Rome, who spread Christianity in the south. St Augustine became the first <u>Archbishop</u> of Canterbury (see pages 162–163 for more about the Archbishop of Canterbury and the Church in Britain today). 🏴

Find out more

© R. Formidable / Shutterstock.com

There are many legends about St Patrick and St Colomba. People believed that St Patrick ordered all the snakes to leave Ireland and that is why there are no native snakes in that country.

You may have heard about the Scottish Loch Ness monster. The first story of this animal is in the life of St Columba in the 6th century. St Columba stopped the monster from attacking a man swimming across the River Ness. The local people were so impressed that they agreed to become Christians.

Check your learning

3.5 Which of the following saints was the first Archbishop of Canterbury?

- ☐ St Augustine
- ☐ St Colombo
- ☐ St David
- ☐ St Patrick

 ## NOTE

St is the short form of 'saint', used before a name.

The Vikings

The Vikings came from Denmark and Norway. They first visited Britain in AD 789 to <u>raid</u> coastal towns and take away goods and slaves. Then, they began to stay and form their own communities in the east of England and Scotland. The Anglo-Saxon kingdoms in England united under King Alfred the Great, who defeated the Vikings. Many of the Viking invaders stayed in Britain — especially in the east and north of England, in an area known as the Danelaw (many place names there, such as Grimsby and Scunthorpe, come from the

© Everett Collection / Shutterstock.com

Viking longship

Viking languages). The Viking settlers mixed with local communities and some converted to Christianity.

Anglo-Saxon kings continued to rule what is now England, except for a short period when there were Danish kings. The first of these was Cnut, also called Canute.

In the north, the people were frightened of a Viking attack so they came together under one king, Kenneth MacAlpin. The term Scotland began to be used to describe that country.

Check your learning

3.6 What nationality was Kenneth MacAlpin?

- ☐ Anglo-Saxon
- ☐ Scottish
- ☐ Viking

Find out more

King Cnut had his chair carried down to the seashore and ordered the waves to go back off his land. Of course, his orders were ignored. He did this to 'Let all the world know that the power of kings is empty and worthless' and that the only king with real power was God.

Find out more

When King Alfred was fleeing from the Vikings, a peasant woman gave him shelter. She asked him to watch some cakes baking in the oven. Alfred, worrying about the problems of his kingdom, let the cakes burn. When the woman – who did not know he was the king – came back, she scolded him. Alfred said how sorry he was and promised to take better care of her cooking in the future.

King Alfred the Great statue, Winchester

© Gary James Calder / Shutterstock.com

🇬🇧 The Norman Conquest

In 1066, an invasion led by William, the Duke of Normandy (in what is now northern France), defeated Harold, the Saxon king of England, at the Battle of Hastings. Harold was killed in the battle. William became king of England and is known as William the Conqueror. The battle is <u>commemorated</u> in a great piece of embroidery, known as the Bayeux Tapestry, which can still be seen in France today.

The Norman Conquest was the last successful foreign invasion of England and led to many changes in government and social structures in England. Norman French, the language of the new ruling class, influenced the development of the English language as we know it today. <u>Initially</u> the Normans also conquered Wales, but the Welsh gradually won their land back. The Scots and the Normans fought on the border between England and Scotland; the Normans took over some land on the border but did not invade Scotland.

William sent people all over England to draw up lists of all the towns and villages. The people who lived there, who owned the land and what animals they owned were also listed. This was called the Domesday Book. It still exists today and gives a picture of society in England just after the Norman Conquest. 🇬🇧

© Duncan Walker / istockphoto

Section of the Bayeux Tapestry

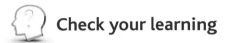

Check your learning

3.7 Is the statement below **True** or **False**?

The Bayeux Tapestry tells the story of the Battle of Hastings in embroidery.

Study tip

Rhymes can help you to remember dates and facts; for example:

At the Battle of Hastings in 1066
William the Conqueror played some tricks.

Find out more

The Domesday book is kept in the National Archives in Kew, London. You can find out more about the Domesday book and see what it says about the area where you live here:
www.nationalarchives.gov.uk/domesday

Study tip

You can use a timeline to remind you of important dates. We have started one for you on the next page. Fill in the blank spaces. It may help to write down what was happening at that time in the country you came from or other countries you know well.

Key events in the UK	Periods and dates	Key events in the country you came from
Early Britain		
Britain separated from the continent of Europe	About 10,000 years ago	
First farmers in Britain Stonehenge Skara Brae	About .... years ago	
Start of the .... Age	About 4,000 years ago	
Start of the .... Age Maiden Castle First coins minted	About 750 BC	
The Romans Julius Caesar failed to invade	55 BC	
Emperor .... invaded Britain	AD 43	
.............., Queen of the Iceni, fought the Romans	AD	
The Romans left Britain	AD	
The Anglo-Saxons Anglo-Saxon kingdoms established in Britain	AD	
Christian missionaries arrived in Britain	AD	
The Vikings First Viking invasions	AD	
Anglo-Saxon kingdoms unite under King	AD	
In .... people unite under Kenneth McAlpin	AD	
The .... Conquest Battle of Hastings	AD	
.............., Duke of ...., defeated the Anglo-Saxon King Harold	AD	
The .... Book was written	AD	

Check your understanding

Now that you have finished Section 1, look at the list below and write down brief notes about the following:

- Early Britain: the people who first lived here, the buildings they left behind and some of the objects they made
- Britain in Roman times: emperors, a queen who fought them, Roman remains
- The Anglo-Saxons, the spread of the Christian religion
- The Vikings
- The Norman Conquest, the changes the Normans made in England and their wars with Scotland and Wales

Study tip

Telling someone else what you have read will help you to remember the information. If there is no-one you can tell, pretend you have to give a talk to students and practise what you are going to say in front of a mirror. Saying it aloud can also help you remember.

SECTION 2 The Middle Ages

In this section you will read about:

- wars fought in Britain and overseas
- the Black Death
- legal and political changes which led to the development of Parliament
- the development of a national culture and identity
- the civil war known as the Wars of the Roses

Find out more

The *Pale* or the *English Pale* was the part of Ireland that was controlled by the English at different times during the Middle Ages. The word 'pale' comes from the Latin word *palus*, meaning a fence. At first, the English built a barrier, or *pale*, between themselves and the Irish tribes who were their enemies. This led to the phrase *'beyond the pale'* to describe behaviour you do not approve of.

War at home and abroad

The period after the Norman Conquest up until about 1485 is called the Middle Ages (or the medieval period). It was a time of almost constant war.

The English kings fought with the Welsh, Scottish and Irish noblemen for control of their lands. In Wales, the English were able to establish their rule. In 1284 King Edward I of England introduced the Statute of Rhuddlan, which annexed Wales to the Crown of England. Huge castles, including Conwy and Caernarvon, were built to maintain this power. By the middle of the 15th century the last Welsh rebellions had been defeated. English laws and the English language were introduced.

In Scotland, the English kings were less successful. In 1314 the Scottish, led by Robert the Bruce, defeated the English at the Battle of Bannockburn, and Scotland remained unconquered by the English.

At the beginning of the Middle Ages, Ireland was an independent country. The English first went to Ireland as soldiers to help the Irish king and remained to build their own settlements. By 1200, the English ruled an area of Ireland known as the Pale, around Dublin. Some of the important lords in other parts of Ireland accepted the authority of the English king.

During the Middle Ages, the English kings also fought a number of wars abroad. Many knights took part in the Crusades, in which European Christians fought for control of the Holy Land. English kings also fought a long war with France, called the Hundred Years War (even though it actually lasted 116 years). One of the most famous battles of the Hundred Years War was the Battle of Agincourt in 1415, where King Henry V's vastly outnumbered English army defeated the French. The English left France in the 1450s.

Find out more

The Holy Land is the area in the Middle East around Jerusalem, now in modern Israel and Palestine. It is holy to three world religions which started here: Judaism, Christianity and Islam. European kings fought many wars, called crusades, over hundreds of years to try and take the land from its Muslim rulers and bring it under Christian control.

Check your learning

3.8 Are the following statements **True** or **False**?

A King Edward used the Statute of Rhuddlan to take over Wales, where he built huge castles.

B By the year 1200 the Kings of England ruled over Ireland, Scotland and Wales.

3.9 Without looking at the text, can you remember the name of the king who won the Battle of Agincourt during the Hundred Years War?

Find out more

According to a legend the Welsh asked Edward I for 'a prince born in Wales, who did not speak a word of English'. To their surprise he agreed and then presented his infant son, later Edward II, who was born in Caernarfon Castle.

The Black Death

The Normans used a system of land ownership known as feudalism. The king gave land to his lords in return for help in war. Landowners had to send certain numbers of men to serve in the army. Some <u>peasants</u> had their own land but most were <u>serfs</u>. They had a small area of their lord's land where they could grow food. In return, they had to work for their lord and could not move away. The same system developed in southern Scotland. In the north of Scotland and Ireland, land was owned by members of the 'clans' (<u>prominent</u> families).

In 1348, a disease, probably a form of <u>plague</u>, came to Britain. This was known as the Black Death. One third of the population of England died and a similar proportion in Scotland and Wales. This was one of the worst disasters ever to strike Britain. Following the Black Death, the smaller population meant there was less need to grow cereal crops. There were labour shortages and peasants began to demand higher wages. New social classes appeared, including owners of large areas of land (later called the gentry), and people left the countryside to live in the towns. In the towns, growing wealth led to the development of a strong middle class.

In Ireland, the Black Death killed many in the Pale and, for a time, the area controlled by the English became smaller.

Find out more

A plague is a terrible disease that spreads easily and kills a lot of people quickly. The Black Death, or bubonic plague, is thought to have started in east or central Asia. Fleas found on black rats that lived on ships probably carried the disease to Europe and gave it to humans.

Study tip

Use the power of your imagination when learning facts and figures. You could imagine a giant black rat with evil eyes and pointed teeth wearing a collar with the number 1348 on it. Fleas jumping off its back could be heading towards peasants in the fields or people in the street. You could draw it in your notebook.

Black rat
© Pelevina Ksinia / Shutterstock.com

Check your learning

3.10 Tick the boxes beside the names of two places where feudalism existed:

☐ England   ☐ Ireland   ☐ South of Scotland   ☐ North of Scotland

🏴 Legal and political changes

In the Middle Ages, Parliament began to develop into the <u>institution</u> it is today. Its origins can be traced to the king's council of advisers, which included important noblemen and the leaders of the Church.

There were few formal limits to the king's power until 1215. In that year, King John was forced by his noblemen to agree to a number of demands. The result was a <u>charter</u> of rights called the Magna Carta (which means the Great Charter). The Magna Carta established the idea that even the king was <u>subject to</u> the law. It protected the rights of the <u>nobility</u> and restricted the king's power to collect taxes or to make or change laws. In future, the king would need to involve his <u>noblemen</u> in decisions.

In England, parliaments were called for the king to consult his nobles, particularly when the king needed to raise money. The numbers attending Parliament increased and two separate parts, known as Houses, were established. The nobility, great landowners and <u>bishops</u> sat in the House of Lords. Knights, who were usually smaller landowners, and wealthy people from towns and cities were elected to sit in the <u>House of Commons</u>. Only a small part of the population was able to join in electing the members of the Commons.

A similar Parliament developed in Scotland. It had three Houses, called Estates: the lords, the commons and the <u>clergy</u>.

This was also a time of development in the <u>legal</u> system. The principle that judges are independent of the government began to be established. In England, judges developed 'common law' by a process of precedence (that is, following previous decisions) and tradition. In Scotland, the legal system developed slightly differently and laws were 'codified' (that is, written down).

Check your learning

3.11 Complete the following sentence:

> The Magna Carta contains a list of rights that King _____ gave to his noblemen in the year _____.

Study tip

To help you remember details about the Magna Carta, you could imagine a picture. King John is sitting at a table surrounded by noblemen dressed in armour and carrying weapons. One of the nobles is handing him a pen to sign a very long document. At the top of the document are the words 'Laws the King must obey ......' and at the bottom the words 'sign here' and the date 1215. There could be a large clock above the king's head with the time at 12:15.

🏴 A distinct identity

The Middle Ages saw the development of a national culture and identity. After the Norman Conquest, the king and his noblemen had spoken Norman French and the peasants had continued to speak Anglo-Saxon. Gradually these two languages combined to become one English language. Some words in modern English — for example, 'park' and 'beauty' — are based on Norman French words. Others — for example, 'apple', 'cow' and 'summer' — are based on Anglo-Saxon words. In modern English there are often two words with very similar meanings, one from French and one from Anglo-Saxon. 'Demand' (French) and 'ask' (Anglo-Saxon) are examples. By 1400, in England, official documents were being written in English, and English had become the preferred language of the royal court and Parliament.

In the years leading up to 1400, Geoffrey Chaucer wrote a series of poems in English about a group of people going to Canterbury on a <u>pilgrimage</u>. The people decided to tell each other stories on the journey, and the poems describe the travellers and some of the stories they told. This collection of poems is called *The Canterbury Tales*. It was one of the first books to be printed by William Caxton, the first person in England to print books using a printing press. Many of the stories are still popular. Some have been made into plays and television programmes.

In Scotland, many people continued to speak Gaelic and the Scots language also developed. A number of poets began to write in the Scots language. One example is John Barbour, who wrote *The Bruce* about the Battle of Bannockburn.

The Middle Ages also saw a change in the type of buildings in Britain. Castles were built in many places in Britain and Ireland, partly for defence. Today many are in ruins, although some, such as Windsor and Edinburgh, are still in use. Great cathedrals — for example, Lincoln Cathedral — were also built, and many of these are still used for worship. Several of the cathedrals had windows of stained glass, telling stories about the Bible and Christian saints. The glass in York Minster is a famous example.

During this period, England was an important trading nation. English wool became a very important export. People came to England from abroad to trade and also to work. Many had special skills, such as weavers from France, engineers from Germany, glass manufacturers from Italy and canal builders from Holland.

Part of Windsor Castle

Check your learning

3.12 Complete the following sentence:

By 1400 _____ replaced Norman French in Parliament and the royal court in England.

3.13 In what language did John Barbour write a poem about the Battle of Bannockburn?

☐ English ☐ Gaelic ☐ Norman French ☐ Scots

Find out more

Geoffrey Chaucer is known as the father of English literature and the greatest English poet of the Middle Ages. He was very popular at the court of King Richard II but died suddenly and some people believe that enemies of the king, who was also killed, murdered him.

Find out more

Robert the Bruce was defeated many times by the English army. There is a story that he once took shelter in cave after losing yet another battle. He was ready to give up and leave Scotland. He suddenly saw a little spider trying to swing from one wall of the cave to another. It missed and missed again six times, but the seventh time it reached and was able to make a web. Robert the Bruce took this as a sign – he too had lost six battles. His courage returned, he gathered his supporters together and went on to win back Scottish independence from the English king at Bannockburn.

i NOTE

There are many kings and queens with the same name. To avoid confusion we add a number to their name. These numbers are written using Roman numerals. The present queen is the second with the name Elizabeth. We call her Queen Elizabeth the Second and write her name as Queen Elizabeth II.

1	I	5	V
2	II	6	VI
3	III	7	VII
4	IV	8	VIII

Figure 3.1 Roman numerals

The Wars of the Roses

In 1455, a civil war was begun to decide who should be king of England. It was fought between the supporters of two families: the <u>House</u> of Lancaster and the House of York. This war was called the Wars of the Roses, because the symbol of Lancaster was a red rose and the symbol of York was a white rose. The war ended with the Battle of Bosworth Field in 1485. King Richard III of the House of York was killed in the battle and Henry Tudor, the leader of the House of Lancaster, became King Henry VII. Henry then married King Richard's niece, Elizabeth of York, and united the two families. Henry was the first king of the House of Tudor. The symbol of the House of Tudor was a red rose with a white rose inside it as a sign that the Houses of York and Lancaster were now <u>allies</u>.

Check your learning

3.14 The Wars of the Roses began in 1455. When did they end?

☐ 1465   ☐ 1475   ☐ 1485   ☐ 1495

3.15 What were names of the two families fighting against each other in the Wars of the Roses?

☐ House of Gloucester   ☐ House of Lancaster

☐ House of York   ☐ House of Kent

Find out more

Archaeologists discovered that bones found underneath a city council car park in Leicester in February 2013 belonged to Richard III of the House of York.

© Georgios Kollidas / Shutterstock.com

Check your understanding – The Middle Ages

Now that you have read Section 2, what can you remember about the following?

■ The many wars fought during the Middle Ages in Britain, Ireland and overseas

■ The system of land ownership

■ The effects of the Black Death on society

■ The development of parliaments in England and Scotland

■ The development of an English language and cultural identity

■ The Wars of the Roses

■ The beginning of the Tudor <u>dynasty</u>

Study tip

There is a timeline on the next page to help you to remember the dates in this section like the one at the end of Section 1. We have started it for you. Fill in the blank spaces. It may help to write down what was happening in the country you came from at around the same time.

Key events in the UK	Periods and dates	Key events in the country you came from
1200–1400		
The English ruled the land called the Pale around .... in Ireland	By 1200	
Statute of Rhuddlan, Edward I took over Wales	....	
.... won the Battle of Bannockburn	1314	
The start of the Black Death	....	
1400–1500		
Chaucer's poems printed in English by	1400s	
Henry V won the Battle of Agincourt	1415	
Start of the Wars of the Roses	1455	
Battle of .... ended the Wars of the Roses	....	

SECTION 3 The Tudors and Stuarts

In this section you will read about:

- changes in religion and some reasons why they happened
- Henry VIII, his six wives and three children
- poetry and drama in the Elizabethan period and 16th and 17th centuries
- what British kings did in Ireland
- when England was a republic
- the development of Parliament
- the restoration of the monarchy
- the Glorious Revolution

🇬🇧 Religious conflicts

After his victory in the Wars of the Roses, Henry VII wanted to make sure that England remained peaceful and that his position as king was secure. He deliberately strengthened the central administration of England and reduced the power of the nobles. He was <u>thrifty</u> and built up the monarchy's financial reserves. When he died, his son Henry VIII continued the policy of <u>centralising power</u>.

Henry VIII was most famous for breaking away from the Church of Rome and marrying six times.

To divorce his first wife, Henry needed the approval of the <u>Pope</u>. When the Pope refused, Henry established the Church of England. In this new Church, the king, not the Pope, would have the power to appoint bishops and order how people should worship.

At the same time the <u>Reformation</u> was happening across Europe. This was a movement against the authority of the Pope and the ideas and practices of the Roman Catholic Church. The <u>Protestants</u> formed their own churches. They read the Bible in their own languages instead of in Latin; they did not pray to saints or at <u>shrines</u>; and they believed that a person's own relationship with God was more important than <u>submitting</u> to the authority of the Church. Protestant ideas gradually gained strength in England, Wales and Scotland during the 16th century.

In Ireland, however, attempts by the English to impose Protestantism (alongside efforts to introduce the English system of laws about the inheritance of land) led to rebellion from the Irish <u>chieftains</u>, and much brutal fighting followed.

During the reign of Henry VIII, Wales became formally united with England by the Act for the Government of Wales. The Welsh sent representatives to the House of Commons and the Welsh legal system was reformed.

Henry VIII was <u>succeeded</u> by his son Edward VI, who was strongly Protestant. During his reign, the Book of Common Prayer was written to be used in the Church of England. A version of this book is still used in some churches today. Edward died at the age of 15 after ruling for just over six years, and his half-sister Mary became queen. Mary was a <u>devout</u> Catholic and persecuted Protestants (for this reason, she became known as 'Bloody Mary'). Mary also died after a short reign and the next monarch was her half-sister, Elizabeth, the daughter of Henry VIII and Anne Boleyn.

British stamps showing King Henry VIII and his six wives

© Neftali / Shutterstock.com

Queen Elizabeth I was a Protestant. She re-established the Church of England as the official Church in England. Everyone had to attend their local church and there were laws about the type of religious services and the prayers which could be said, but Elizabeth did not ask about people's real beliefs. She succeeded in finding a balance between the views of Catholics and the more extreme Protestants. In this way, she avoided any serious religious conflict within England. Elizabeth became one of the most popular monarchs in English history, particularly after 1588, when the English defeated the Spanish Armada (a large fleet of ships), which had been sent by Spain to conquer England and restore Catholicism.

Check your learning

3.16 Which of the following kings broke away from the Church of Rome and established the Church of England?

☐ Henry VII
☐ Henry VIII

Find out more

The Reformation gets its name from the movements across Europe to **reform** or change the Catholic Church. Many people throughout society wanted to read the Bible in their own language, not in Latin, so that they could understand what it said. Before this, no one was allowed to translate the Bible.

People who wanted to reform the Catholic Church were called Protestants because they were **protesting** against the Pope, the head of the Church, and his laws.

⊞ The six wives of Henry VIII

Catherine of Aragon – Catherine was a Spanish princess. She and Henry had a number of children but only one, Mary, survived. When Catherine was too old to give him another child, Henry decided to divorce her, hoping that another wife would give him a son to be his <u>heir</u>.

Anne Boleyn – Anne Boleyn was English. She and Henry had one daughter, Elizabeth. Anne was unpopular in the country and was accused of taking lovers. She was <u>executed</u> at the Tower of London.

Jane Seymour – Henry married Jane after Anne's execution. She gave Henry the son he wanted, Edward, but she died shortly after the birth.

Anne of Cleves – Anne was a German princess. Henry married her for political reasons but divorced her soon after.

Catherine Howard – Catherine was a cousin of Anne Boleyn. She was also accused of taking lovers and executed.

Catherine Parr – Catherine was a widow who married Henry late in his life. She survived him and married again but died soon after. ⊞

Study tip

Here are a couple of mnemonic verses to help you remember about King Henry VIII's wives.

King Henry the Eighth,
to six wives he was wedded.
One died, one survived,
two divorced, two beheaded.

The following verse tells you the order in which he married and separated from his wives:

Divorced, beheaded, died,
Divorced, beheaded, survived.
I'm Henry the Eighth, I had six sorry wives
Some might say I ruined their lives.

Check your learning

3.17 Without looking at the text can you write down the names of the child of each of these queens?

Catherine of Aragon was the mother of _____

Anne Boleyn was the mother of _____

Jane Seymour was the mother of _____

The Reformation in Scotland and Mary, Queen of Scots

Scotland had also been strongly influenced by Protestant ideas. In 1560, the predominantly Protestant Scottish Parliament abolished the authority of the Pope in Scotland and Roman Catholic religious services became illegal. A Protestant Church of Scotland with an elected leadership was established but, unlike in England, this was not a state Church.

The queen of Scotland, Mary Stuart (often now called 'Mary, Queen of Scots') was a Catholic. She was only a week old when her father died and she became queen. Much of her childhood was spent in France. When she returned to Scotland, she was the centre of a power struggle between different groups. When her husband was murdered, Mary was suspected of involvement and fled to England. She gave her throne to her Protestant son, James VI of Scotland. Mary was Elizabeth I's cousin and hoped that Elizabeth might help her, but Elizabeth suspected Mary of wanting to take over the English throne, and kept her a prisoner for 20 years. Mary was eventually executed, accused of plotting against Elizabeth I.

Check your learning

3.18 The Scottish Parliament made Roman Catholic services illegal in the country in

☐ 1525 ☐ 1560 ☐ 1575 ☐ 1590

3.19 Mary, Queen of Scots was Elizabeth I's

☐ mother ☐ sister ☐ aunt ☐ cousin

© Georgios Kollidas / Shutterstock.com

Find out more

After killing her, the executioner held up Mary's head and said, 'God save the Queen'. At that moment, he dropped her head and the lovely auburn hair in his hand turned out to be a wig, revealing that Mary had very short, grey hair.

Portrait of Mary, Queen of Scots

🇬🇧 Exploration, poetry and drama

The Elizabethan period in England was a time of growing patriotism: a feeling of pride in being English. English explorers sought new trade routes and tried to expand British trade into the Spanish colonies in the Americas. Sir Francis Drake, one of the commanders in the defeat of the Spanish Armada, was one of the founders of England's naval tradition. His ship, the *Golden Hind*, was one of the first to sail right around ('circumnavigate') the world. In Elizabeth I's time, English settlers first began to <u>colonise</u> the eastern coast of America.

This colonisation, particularly by people who disagreed with the religious views of the next two kings, greatly increased in the next century.

The Elizabethan period is also remembered for the richness of its poetry and drama, especially the plays and poems of William Shakespeare. 🇬🇧

Check your learning

3.20 Are the following statements **True** or **False**?

A English people started to colonise the eastern coast of America in the time of Elizabeth I.

B Sir Frances Drake was in America at the time of the Spanish Armada in 1588.

Find out more

Queen Elizabeth I refused to marry and be ruled by a husband. She was a strong ruler able to control powerful male nobles. She made a famous speech to her soldiers before the battle with the Spanish Armada saying: 'I know I have the body of a weak and feeble woman; but I have the heart and stomach of a king, and of a king of England too'. She added that if the Spanish won the sea battle, she was willing to lead her army as its general.

Find out more

There is a story that Sir Francis Drake was playing bowls when he was warned that the Spanish fleet had been seen sailing towards England. He replied that there was plenty of time to finish his game and still beat the Spanish.

Replica of the Golden Hind

🇬🇧 William Shakespeare (1564–1616)

Shakespeare was born in Stratford-upon-Avon, England. He was a playwright and actor and wrote many poems and plays. His most famous plays include *A Midsummer Night's Dream*, *Hamlet*, *Macbeth* and *Romeo and Juliet*. He also <u>dramatised</u> significant events from the past, but he did not focus solely on kings and queens. He was one of the first to portray ordinary Englishmen and women. Shakespeare had a great influence on the English language and invented many words that are still common today. Lines from his plays and poems that are often still quoted include:

> Once more unto the breach (*Henry V*)
> To be or not to be (*Hamlet*)
> A rose by any other name (*Romeo and Juliet*)
> All the world's a stage (*As You Like It*)
> The darling buds of May (<u>Sonnet</u> 18 – *Shall I Compare Thee To A Summer's Day*).

Many people regard Shakespeare as the greatest playwright of all time. His plays and poems are still performed and studied in Britain and other countries today. The Globe Theatre in London is a modern copy of the theatres in which his plays were first performed. 🇬🇧

The Globe Theatre, London

© Lance Bellers / Shutterstock.com

Check your learning

3.21 Name two of Shakespeare's plays mentioned in the text.

1. _____

2. _____

3.22 Where is the modern copy of The Globe Theatre?

☐ Stratford-upon-Avon   ☐ Birmingham

☐ London   ☐ York

James VI and I

Elizabeth I never married and so had no children of her own to inherit her throne. When she died in 1603 her heir was her cousin James VI of Scotland. He became King James I of England, Wales and Ireland but Scotland remained a separate country.

The King James Bible

One achievement of King James' reign was a new translation of the Bible into English. This translation is known as the 'King James Version' or the 'Authorised Version'. It was not the first English Bible but is a version which continues to be used in many Protestant churches today.

Check your learning

3.23 Is the following statement **True** or **False**?

When James inherited Elizabeth I's throne in 1603, England, Ireland, Scotland and Wales become one country.

Find out more

King James chose about 50 scholars from the Church of England, who were based in London, Oxford and Cambridge, to rewrite the Bible. They worked in six groups to translate different parts of early texts of the Bible from Greek and Hebrew into English.

 Ireland

During this period, Ireland was an almost completely Catholic country. Henry VII and Henry VIII had extended English control outside the Pale (see pages 44–45) and had established English authority over the whole country. Henry VIII took the title 'King of Ireland'. English laws were introduced and local leaders were expected to follow the instructions of the Lord Lieutenants in Dublin.

During the reigns of Elizabeth I and James I, many people in Ireland opposed rule by the Protestant government in England. There were a number of rebellions. The English government encouraged Scottish and English Protestants to settle in Ulster, the northern province of Ireland, taking over the land from Catholic landholders. These settlements were known as plantations. Many of the new settlers came from south-west Scotland and other land was given to companies based in London. James later organised similar plantations in several other parts of Ireland. This had serious long-term consequences for the history of England, Scotland and Ireland.

Check your learning

3.24 Which of the following British Kings called himself King of Ireland?

☐ Henry V ☐ Henry VIII

☐ James VI ☐ Richard III

3.25 Complete the following sentence:

The English government encouraged Scottish and English
_____ to settle in Ulster, the northern province of Ireland.
These settlements were called _____.

🇬🇧 The rise of Parliament

Elizabeth I was very skilled at managing Parliament. During her reign, she was successful in balancing her wishes and views against those of the House of Lords and those of the House of Commons, which was increasingly Protestant in its views.

James I and his son Charles I were less skilled politically. Both believed in the 'Divine Right of Kings': the idea that the king was directly appointed by God to rule. They thought that the king should be able to act without having to seek approval from Parliament. When Charles I inherited the thrones of England, Wales, Ireland and Scotland, he tried to rule in line with this principle. When he could not get Parliament to agree with his religious and foreign policies, he tried to rule without Parliament at all. For 11 years, he found ways in which to raise money without Parliament's approval but eventually trouble in Scotland meant that he had to recall Parliament. 🇬🇧

Find out more

Guy Fawkes and a group of English Catholics planned to blow up the House of Lords and kill the king during the State Opening of Parliament on 5 November 1605. This was to be the start of a rebellion. Guy Fawkes, who was in charge of the explosives, was arrested before he did any damage. His failure is celebrated on Bonfire Night on 5 November (see page 171).

Check your learning

3.26 Without looking at the text, complete the following sentence:

James I and Charles I believed that they were chosen by _____ to rule.

🏴 The beginning of the English Civil War

Charles I wanted the worship of the Church of England to include more ceremony and introduced a revised Prayer Book. He tried to impose this Prayer Book on the Presbyterian Church in Scotland and this led to serious unrest. A Scottish army was formed and Charles could not find the money he needed for his own army without the help of Parliament. In 1640, he recalled Parliament to ask it for funds. Many in Parliament were Puritans, a group of Protestants who <u>advocated</u> strict and simple religious <u>doctrine</u> and worship. They did not agree with the king's religious views and disliked his reforms of the Church of England. Parliament refused to give the king the money he asked for, even after the Scottish army invaded England.

Another rebellion began in Ireland because the Roman Catholics in Ireland were afraid of the growing power of the Puritans. Parliament took this opportunity to demand control of the English army – a change that would have transferred substantial power from the king to Parliament. In response, Charles I entered the House of Commons and tried to arrest five parliamentary leaders, but they had been warned and were not there. (No monarch has set foot in the Commons since.) <u>Civil war</u> between the king and Parliament could not now be avoided and began in 1642. The country split into those who supported the king (the Cavaliers) and those who supported Parliament (the Roundheads). 🏴

Check your learning

3.27 When did the civil war between King Charles I and Parliament begin in England?

☐ 1634   ☐ 1642   ☐ 1650   ☐ 1656

3.28 Which of the following statements is correct?

A The Puritans who opposed King Charles were a group of Protestants.
B The Puritans who opposed King Charles were a group of Roman Catholics.

Find out more

Puritans were Protestants who wanted a 'purer' form of religion. They wanted church services to be simple and different from those of the Catholic Church. They did not want the rule of bishops, or statues and pictures of saints. They banned music, dancing and celebrations on feast and saints' days. Puritans wore very plain clothes; women had simple hairstyles and wore plain head coverings. Parliament's army was called the Roundheads because their hair was cut very short.

The King's supporters, called Royalists or Cavaliers, wore their hair long and curled. Their church services were very similar to Catholic ones, with singing and incense but in English, not Latin. They enjoyed music in church, sang, danced and celebrated feast days. Their clothes were colourful with embroidery, lace and ribbons.

⊞ Oliver Cromwell and the English republic

The king's army was defeated at the Battles of Marston Moor and Naseby. By 1646, it was clear that Parliament had won the war. Charles was held prisoner by the parliamentary army. He was still unwilling to reach any agreement with Parliament and in 1649 he was executed.

England declared itself a republic, called the Commonwealth. It no longer had a monarch. For a time, it was not totally clear how the country would be governed. For now, the army was in control. One of its generals, Oliver Cromwell, was sent to Ireland where the revolt, which had begun in 1641, still continued and where there was still a Royalist army. Cromwell was successful in establishing the authority of the English Parliament but did this with such violence that even today Cromwell remains a <u>controversial</u> figure in Ireland.

The Scots had not agreed to the execution of Charles I and declared his son Charles II to be king. He was crowned king of Scotland and led a Scottish army into England. Cromwell defeated this army in the Battles of Dunbar and Worcester. Charles II escaped from Worcester, famously hiding in an oak tree on one occasion, and eventually fled to Europe. Parliament now controlled Scotland as well as England and Wales.

After his campaign in Ireland and victory over Charles II at Worcester, Cromwell was recognised as the leader of the new republic. He was given the title of Lord Protector and ruled until his death in 1658. When Cromwell died, his son, Richard, became Lord Protector in his place but was not able to control the army or the government. Although Britain had been a republic for 11 years, without Oliver Cromwell there was no clear leader or system of government. Many people in the country wanted stability. People began to talk about the need for a king.

Find out more

Oliver Cromwell encouraged Jews to return to England in 1657, over 350 years after Edward I made them leave. Historians believe that Cromwell hoped that they would convert to Christianity. Although Jews, and other Christian sects such as Quakers, were allowed to follow their religion, the Church of England and Catholicism were forbidden.

© Georgios Kollidas / Shutterstock.com

 ## Check your learning

3.29 A Can you name one of the battles that King Charles I's army lost?

_____

B And one of the battles that the Scottish army lost?

_____

3.30 Complete the following sentences:

By 1646, it was clear that _____ had won the war.

_____ would not agree with anything Parliament wanted and in 1649 he was _____.

3.31 Who did the Scots declare king?

☐ Oliver Cromwell ☐ Charles I

☐ Charles II ☐ Richard Cromwell

Find out more

The republic of England was far from democratic. Cromwell abolished the House of Lords and ruled with the help of Puritans who supported his army. There were groups of politicians who wanted real changes, including the vote for all men, greater equality, religious tolerance and free elections. One group, called the 'Diggers', wanted to get rid of private property and own land communally. Cromwell did not agree and dismissed Parliament in 1653. England was governed by a military dictatorship. Cromwell refused the crown but chose his son Richard to become Lord Protector after his death. Military rule was expensive and he raised taxes to pay his army. In Ireland, his army killed thousands of people. He and his army sold land in Northern Ireland to Protestants. Thousands of Irish peasants who had survived the war were sent to the American colonies to work for landowners there.

🏴 The Restoration

In May 1660, Parliament invited Charles II to come back from exile in the Netherlands. He was crowned King Charles II of England, Wales, Scotland and Ireland. Charles II made it clear that he had 'no wish to go on his travels again'. He understood that he could not always do as he wished but would sometimes need to reach agreement with Parliament. Generally, Parliament supported his policies. The Church of England again became the <u>established official Church</u>. Both Roman Catholics and Puritans were kept out of power.

During Charles II's reign, in 1665, there was a major outbreak of plague in London. Thousands of people died, especially in poorer areas. The following year, a great fire destroyed much of the city, including many churches and St Paul's Cathedral. London was rebuilt with a new St Paul's, which was designed by a famous architect, Sir Christopher Wren. Samuel Pepys wrote about these events in a diary which was later published and is still read today.

The Habeas Corpus Act became law in 1679. This was a very important piece of legislation, which remains relevant today. Habeas corpus is Latin for 'you must present the person in court'. The Act guaranteed that no one could be held prisoner unlawfully. Every prisoner has a right to a court hearing.

Charles II was interested in science. During his reign, the Royal Society was formed to promote 'natural knowledge'. This is the oldest surviving scientific society in the world. Among its early members were Sir Edmund Halley, who successfully predicted the return of the comet now called Halley's Comet, and Sir Isaac Newton.

St Paul's Cathedral

Find out more

The Great Fire of London started at a bakery in Pudding Lane and lasted from Sunday 2 September to Wednesday 5 September 1666. It destroyed the homes of around 70,000 of the City's 80,000 inhabitants.

 Check your learning

3.32 Charles II was crowned King of England, Scotland, Wales and Ireland in:

☐ 1649   ☐ 1655   ☐ 1660   ☐ 1675

3.33 Which two of the following disasters happened in London during Charles II's time?

☐ The Great Fire of London   ☐ A great flood

☐ A plague   ☐ The collapse of London Bridge

Find out more

In 1772, James Somersett, a slave bought in Boston and brought to London, was able to use the Habeas Corpus Act to gain his freedom. The man who bought him imprisoned him on a ship leaving for Jamaica where he would be sold to a plantation owner. His friends took his case to court under the Habeas Corpus Act. The judge ordered the ship's captain to bring Somersett to court, and declared that slavery was not lawful in England and Wales and that he must go free.

⊞ Isaac Newton (1643–1727)

Born in Lincolnshire, eastern England, Isaac Newton first became interested in science when he studied at Cambridge University. He became an important figure in the field. His most famous published work was *Philosophiae Naturalis Principia Mathematica* ('Mathematical Principles of Natural Philosophy'), which showed how <u>gravity</u> applied to the whole universe. Newton also discovered that white light is made up of the colours of the rainbow. Many of his discoveries are still important for modern science. ⊞

Find out more

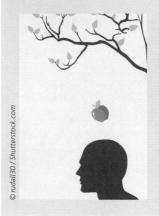

© rudall30 / Shutterstock.com

Sir Isaac Newton himself often told the story that his theory of gravity was inspired by seeing an apple fall from a tree. Although many believe that the apple story was made up and that he did not develop his theory of gravity in a single moment, Newton's acquaintances confirmed the story, although not the story that the apple actually hit Newton's head.

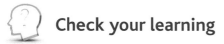 Check your learning

3.34 Can you match the famous men with what they did?

A Sir Isaac Newton ☐ Designed St Paul's Cathedral

B Edmund Halley ☐ Wrote a famous diary

C Christopher Wren ☐ Predicted the return of a comet

D Samuel Pepys ☐ Explained how gravity works

A Catholic king

Charles II had no <u>legitimate children</u>. He died in 1685 and his brother, James, who was a Roman Catholic, became King James II in England, Wales and Ireland and King James VII of Scotland. James favoured Roman Catholics and allowed them to be army officers, which an Act of Parliament had forbidden. He did not seek to reach agreements with Parliament and arrested some of the bishops of the Church of England. People in England worried that James wanted to make England a Catholic country once more. However, his heirs were his two daughters, who were both firmly Protestant, and people thought that this meant there would soon be a Protestant monarch again. Then, James's wife had a son. Suddenly, it seemed likely that the next monarch would not be a Protestant after all.

Check your learning

3.35 Choose A, B or C to complete the following sentences.

When Charles II died in 1685 his _____ James became king.

A cousin   B son   C brother

People in England worried that James, who was a _____, wanted to change the country's religion.

A Catholic   B Presbyterian   C Protestant

Find out more

Today Catholics, and people of any religion, can be army officers or members of parliament. However, the king or queen has to belong to the Church of England.

🏴󠁧󠁢 The Glorious Revolution

James II's elder daughter, Mary, was married to her cousin William of Orange, the Protestant ruler of the Netherlands. In 1688, important Protestants in England asked William to invade England and <u>proclaim</u> himself king. When William reached England, there was no resistance. James fled to France and William took over the throne, becoming William III in England, Wales and Ireland, and William II of Scotland. William ruled jointly with Mary. This event was later called the 'Glorious Revolution' because there was no fighting in England and because it guaranteed the power of Parliament, ending the threat of a monarch ruling on his or her own as he or she wished. James II wanted to regain the throne and invaded Ireland with the help of a French army. William defeated James II at the Battle of the Boyne in Ireland in 1690, an event which is still celebrated by some in Northern Ireland today. William re-conquered Ireland and James fled back to France. Many restrictions were placed on the Roman Catholic Church in Ireland and Irish Catholics were unable to take part in the government.

There was also support for James in Scotland. An attempt at an armed rebellion in support of James was quickly defeated at Killiecrankie. All Scottish <u>clans</u> were required formally to accept William as king by taking an oath. The MacDonalds of Glencoe were late in taking the oath and were all killed. The memory of this massacre meant some Scots distrusted the new government.

Some continued to believe that James was the rightful king, particularly in Scotland. Some joined him in exile in France; others were secret supporters. James' supporters became known as Jacobites. 🏴󠁧󠁢

Find out more

The Highland clans believed in giving shelter to anyone who asked, even their enemies. When a group of soldiers led by Captain Robert Campbell asked the MacDonalds for shelter, they agreed. One night during a snowstorm, the Captain ordered his soldiers to kill the MacDonalds. Some Campbell soldiers were disgusted and helped their hosts to escape but many died in the snow. The memory of the massacre is still strong and the old Clachaig Inn at Glencoe still has the sign on its door, 'No Campbells'.

Check your learning

3.36 Choose two reasons why the arrival of William and Mary to become King and Queen is called the 'Glorious Revolution'.

☐ Because there was no fighting in England

☐ Because there was a huge battle and a great victory

☐ Because England took over The Netherlands

☐ Because it guaranteed the power of Parliament

Study tip

Visit your local museum and find out what was happening near your home at the same time as some of the events mentioned in the study material. If you live in or near Belfast, Cardiff, Edinburgh or London you can visit national and city museums and galleries and learn much more about many of the subjects in the study material – and they are free to visit. There are also many historic houses and prehistoric and industrial sites to see in most areas. Museums, libraries and tourist information offices have information on all of these.

Study tip

There is a timeline on the next page to help you to remember the dates in this section. We have started it for you. Fill in the blank spaces and add your own notes. You can also add other key events you remember that happened at the same time.

Key events in the UK	Periods and dates	Key events in the country you came from
1500s		
Christians from all over Europe start to break away from the Roman Catholic Church. This was called the R...............	Before and during the 1500s	
The Protestant Church of England is established	First by Henry VIII, then again by Elizabeth I	
The Scottish Parliament established a Protestant Church of Scotland	....	
The English navy defeated the Spanish	1588	
.... wrote some of the best English plays and poems	At the time of Elizabeth I until his death in 1616	
Elizabeth I died and .... becomes King of England, Scotland and Ireland.	1603	
Parliament refused to give .... money to pay his soldiers.	1640	
Rebellion in	1641	
Beginning of the Civil War in England	....	
Parliament .... the Civil War	1646	
Execution of	1649	
Death of ...., Lord Protector	1658	
Charles II became king	....	
The Habeas Corpus Act became law	....	
Death of Charles I;. .... became king	1685	
The Glorious Revolution; .... and .... are crowned	....	
Battle of	1690	

Study tip

Memory journey

This is a very powerful method for remembering lists of any kind. It is based on the idea of remembering landmarks on a 'journey' you know well and linking each one to an item on your list. This could be as simple as walking around a room in your home, your route to the shops, to visit someone or to work, or travelling from one city to another.

How to create and use a memory journey

1 Start by preparing your journey to fix the landmarks in your mind. Shut your eyes and think of the landmarks you remember. Write them down in order on a piece of paper. For example, if it's a route from your home to the supermarket, your list of landmarks might look like this: *Front door, postbox, corner shop, school across the road, post office, bus stop, hairdresser, coffee shop, car wash, traffic lights, supermarket.*

2 Next link these landmarks with the dates and facts you want to remember from the timeline. Imagine them as pictures or images and make this as colourful and funny as you can. Try to use your other senses as well – imagine how they feel, sound and smell wherever you can. Some people believe you should make them pleasant, not horrible, as the brain often blocks out unpleasant images. So if you are trying to remember a battle, you may not want to think about the wounding and killing but instead think of the winners celebrating and the coming of peace.

3 The next page has an example using the events from the timeline – you could draw an image for each one in the margins.

4 You could combine this memory journey with some of the mnemonics mentioned in Chapter 1 Section 5; for example, the tips for remembering dates.

Landmark	Imagine
Front door	Your front door with 1500 written in old numbers, with sweet-smelling Tudor roses growing round it.
Post box	A post box with a church made of clay on the top. Henry VIII and Anne Boleyn standing on either side forming and reforming it into different shaped churches.
Corner shop	A tartan 1560 above the shop door. Protestant bibles and prayer books for sale. Mary, Queen of Scots being taken out as a prisoner. Pictures and broken statues of Catholic saints thrown into a pile.
School grounds	A match between Spanish and English teams, a huge scoreboard as in rugby or cricket above their heads – 15 to the Spanish and 88 to the English.
Post office	Shakespeare with piles of letters and handwritten books, actors from any of the plays you know in the queue - for example, Romeo and Juliet with cards with hearts on them.
Bus stop	James VI/I standing at a bus stop with an indicator board with 'The next bus to England at 16:03' in red lights. He could be carrying a book with My Bible written on the cover.
Hairdresser	Men in colourful fancy clothes having their long hair curled, on the other side are men in plain clothes having their heads shaved or hair cut very short. They are facing each other looking very cross and making rude signs. King Charles has a bill for £16.40 and is asking a Roundhead for money to pay it. The Roundhead is saying NO very loudly. A price list in the window says: *Special Offers* *Irish Rebellion* 16.41 *English Civil War* 16.42
Coffee shop	Four people sitting around a table playing cards – the numbers on the cards are 1, 6, 4 and 9. Oliver Cromwell is dressed as a waiter carrying a tray with a cake in the shape of King Charles's head.
Car wash	Cars on fire driving in to the car wash (Fire of London), people and black rats covered in fleas (plague) running around; every time a rat touches a person they fall over and vanish. The rats run into the fire and finally vanish.
Traffic lights	A judge sits on top of the traffic lights, stopping police from taking people to prison. The lights are on red. The judge is waving a document that says Habeas Corpus 1679 in front of them.
Supermarket	There is a big party at the supermarket. Posters advertise the Glorious Revolution. William and Mary with huge crowns on their heads are greeting guests. The supermarket is also advertising 16 oranges for 88 pence (for William of Orange).

5 Once you have created your 'journey' you could tell it to yourself as a story. Try it to see if it helps you remember more.

6 You may want to try this technique on something simple like a shopping list first to see if it works for you.

Check your understanding – the Tudors and Stuarts

Now that you have read Section 3, what can you remember about the following?

- Why Britain broke away from the Roman Catholic church
- Henry VIII, his wives and children
- Religious conflicts in England and Scotland
- Poetry and drama in the 16th and 17th centuries
- Explorers, traders and settlers in the Americas
- What Britain did in Ireland
- Civil War and the execution of a king
- When England was a republic
- The development of Parliament
- The restoration of the monarchy
- The Glorious Revolution in England
- Uprisings in Ireland and Scotland

SECTION 4 A global power

In this section you will read about the following:

■ how Parliament became more powerful and the monarchy less so

■ the events that led to Scotland, England and Wales becoming Great Britain

■ the rebellion led by Bonnie Prince Charlie that began and ended in Scotland

■ some of the great thinkers of the Enlightenment and their ideas

■ the Industrial Revolution and how it changed society

■ the war against Napoleon in Europe

■ the slave trade and how it ended

■ the growth of the British Empire

■ how democracy developed

🏴󠁧󠁢 Constitutional monarchy – the Bill of Rights

At the coronation of William and Mary, a Declaration of Rights was read. This confirmed that the king would no longer be able to raise taxes or administer justice without agreement from Parliament. The balance of power between monarch and Parliament had now permanently changed. The Bill of Rights, 1689, confirmed the rights of Parliament and the limits of the king's power. Parliament took control of who could be monarch and declared that the king or queen must be a Protestant. A new Parliament had to be elected at least every three years (later this became seven years and now it is five years). Every year the monarch had to ask Parliament to renew funding for the army and the navy.

These changes meant that, to be able to govern effectively, the monarch needed to have advisers, or ministers, who would be able to ensure a majority of votes in the House of Commons and the House of Lords. There were two main groups in Parliament, known as the Whigs and the Tories. (The modern Conservative Party is still sometimes referred to as the Tories.) This was the beginning of <u>party politics</u>.

This was also an important time for the development of a free press (newspapers and other publications which are not controlled by the government). From 1695, newspapers were allowed to operate without a government licence. Increasing numbers of newspapers began to be published.

The laws passed after the Glorious Revolution are the beginning of what is called '<u>constitutional monarchy</u>'. The monarch remained very important but was no longer able to insist on particular policies or actions if Parliament did not agree. After William III, the ministers gradually became more important than the monarch but this was not a democracy in the modern sense. The number of people who had the right to vote for members of Parliament was still very small. Only men who owned property of a certain value were able to vote. No women at all had the vote.

Some <u>constituencies</u> were controlled by a single wealthy family. These were called 'pocket boroughs'. Other constituencies had hardly any voters and were called 'rotten boroughs'.

Check your learning

3.37 Which of the following statements is **true**?

A The Bill of Rights signed in 1689 allowed the king to raise taxes without asking Parliament.

B The Bill of Rights signed in 1689 said that the king could not raise taxes without the agreement of Parliament.

Find out more

Old Sarum was the most infamous of the 'pocket boroughs', a parliamentary constituency owned and controlled by a single person (until it was abolished under the Reform Act 1832 – see page 99). The constituency was the site of what had been the original settlement of Salisbury, known as Old Sarum. The population had moved to New Sarum, which then became the cathedral city of Salisbury.

A growing population

This was a time when many people left Britain and Ireland to settle in new colonies in America and elsewhere, but others came to live in Britain. The first Jews to come to Britain since the Middle Ages settled in London in 1656. Between 1680 and 1720 many <u>refugees</u> called Huguenots came from France. They were Protestants and had been persecuted for their religion. Many were educated and skilled and worked as scientists, in banking, or in weaving or other crafts.

Check your learning

3.38 During the 1600s large numbers of people left Britain and Ireland to settle in:

☐ France ☐ The American colonies

☐ The Netherlands ☐ The Middle East

🇬🇧 The Act or Treaty of Union in Scotland

William and Mary's <u>successor</u>, Queen Anne, had no surviving children. This created uncertainty over the succession in England, Wales and Ireland and in Scotland. The Act of Union, known as the <u>Treaty</u> of Union in Scotland, was therefore agreed in 1707, creating the Kingdom of Great Britain. Although Scotland was no longer an independent country, it kept its own legal and education systems and Presbyterian Church.

The Prime Minister

When Queen Anne died in 1714, Parliament chose a German, George I, to be the next king, because he was Anne's nearest Protestant relative. An attempt by Scottish Jacobites to put James II's son on the throne instead was quickly defeated. George I did not speak very good English and this increased his need to rely on his ministers. The most important minister in Parliament became known as the <u>Prime Minister</u>. The first man to be called this was Sir Robert Walpole, who was Prime Minister from 1721 to 1742. 🇬🇧

 Check your learning

3.39 When was the Kingdom of Great Britain created?

☐ 1688   ☐ 1707

☐ 1714   ☐ 1721

3.40 Without looking at the text, can you remember the name of the first Prime Minister in Parliament?

Find out more

The Whigs and Tories opposed each other from the 1680s to the 1850s. The Whigs came together as a group campaigning for a constitutional monarchy. They played a key role in the Glorious Revolution of 1688 and were enemies of the Roman Catholic Stuart kings and pretenders.

⊞ The rebellion of the clans

In 1745 there was another attempt to put a Stuart king back on the throne in place of George I's son, George II. Charles Edward Stuart (<u>Bonnie</u> Prince Charlie), the grandson of James II, landed in Scotland. He was supported by <u>clansmen</u> from the Scottish highlands and raised an army. Charles initially had some successes but was defeated by George II's army at the Battle of Culloden in 1746. Charles escaped back to Europe.

The clans lost a lot of their power and influence after Culloden. Chieftains became landlords if they had the favour of the English king, and clansmen became tenants who had to pay for the land they used.

A process began which became known as the 'Highland Clearances'. Many Scottish landlords destroyed individual small farms (known as 'crofts') to make space for large flocks of sheep and cattle. Evictions became very common in the early 19th century. Many Scottish people left for North America at this time. ⊞

Find out more

Prince Charles Edward Stuart (Bonnie Prince Charlie) fled to the Isle of Skye after his defeat at the Battle of Culloden in 1746. He was helped by a young woman, Flora MacDonald, who dressed him in her maid's clothes. *The Skye Boat Song*, a Scottish folk song, is about this event.

Check your learning

3.41 Which of the following statements is correct?

☐ A Bonnie Prince Charlie lost the Battle of Culloden in 1746 and escaped to Europe.

☐ B Bonnie Prince Charlie was captured at the Battle of Culloden and taken to London.

3.42 Complete the following sentence:

The period when many Scottish landlords destroyed small farms and forced people off their land is called the _____.

 Robert Burns (1759–96)

Known in Scotland as 'The Bard', Robert Burns was a Scottish poet. He wrote in the Scots language, English with some Scottish words, and standard English. He also revised a lot of traditional folk songs by changing or adding lyrics. Burns' best-known work is probably the song *Auld Lang Syne*, which is sung by people in the UK and other countries when they are celebrating the New Year (or Hogmanay as it is called in Scotland).

Find out more

Robert Burns loved many women and wrote some beautiful poetry for them. The following is the first verse of one of his most popular poems:

A Red, Red Rose

O my Luve's like a red, red rose,
   That's newly sprung in June;
O my Luve's like the melodie,
   That's sweetly play'd in tune.

© Naddya / Shutterstock.com

 Check your learning

3.43   When do the Scots celebrate Hogmanay?

The Enlightenment

During the 18th century, new ideas about politics, philosophy and science were developed. This is often called 'the <u>Enlightenment</u>'. Many of the great thinkers of the Enlightenment were Scottish. Adam Smith developed ideas about economics which are still referred to today. David Hume's ideas about human nature continue to influence philosophers. Scientific discoveries, such as James Watt's work on steam power, helped the progress of the Industrial Revolution. One of the most important principles of the Enlightenment was that everyone should have the right to their own political and religious beliefs and that the state should not try to dictate to them. This continues to be an important principle in the UK today.

Check your learning

3.44 Match the following people with the work for which they were famous:

A David Hume   ☐ Steam power

B Adam Smith   ☐ Philosophy

C James Watt   ☐ Economics

The Industrial Revolution

Before the 18th century, agriculture was the biggest source of employment in Britain. There were many cottage industries, where people worked from home to produce goods such as cloth and lace.

The Industrial Revolution was the rapid development of industry in Britain in the 18th and 19th centuries. Britain was the first country to industrialise on a large scale. It happened because of the development of machinery and the use of steam power. Agriculture and the manufacturing of goods became <u>mechanised</u>. This made things more efficient and increased production. Coal and other raw materials were needed to power the new factories. Many people moved from the countryside and started working in the mining and manufacturing industries.

The development of the <u>Bessemer process</u> for the mass production of steel led to the development of the shipbuilding industry and the railways. Manufacturing jobs became the main source of employment in Britain.

Better transport links were needed to transport raw materials and manufactured goods. Canals were built to link the factories to towns and cities and to the ports, particularly in the new industrial areas in the middle and north of England.

Working conditions during the Industrial Revolution were very poor. There were no laws to protect employees, who were often forced to work long hours in dangerous situations. Children also worked and were treated in the same way as adults. Sometimes they were treated even more harshly.

This was also a time of increased colonisation overseas. Captain James Cook mapped the coast of Australia and a few colonies were established there. Britain gained control over Canada, and the East India Company, originally set up to trade, gained control of large parts of India. Colonies began to be established in southern Africa.

Britain traded all over the world and began to import more goods. Sugar and tobacco came from North America and the West Indies; textiles, tea and spices came from India and the area that is today called Indonesia. Trading and settlements overseas sometimes brought Britain into conflict with other countries, particularly France, which was expanding and trading in a similar way in many of the same areas of the world.

Check your learning

3.45 Complete the following sentence:

The Bessemer process was used to produce _____ .

3.46 Is the following sentence **True** or **False**?

Captain James Cook produced a map of the coast of Australia.

⊞ Richard Arkwright (1732–92)

Born in 1732, Arkwright originally trained and worked as a barber. He was able to dye hair and make wigs. When wigs became less popular, he started to work in textiles. He improved the original carding machine. Carding is the process of preparing fibres for spinning into yarn and fabric. He also developed horse-driven spinning mills that used only one machine. This increased the efficiency of production. Later, he used the steam engine to power machinery. Arkwright is particularly remembered for the efficient and profitable way that he ran his factories.

Sake Dean Mahomet (1759–1851)

Mahomet was born in 1759 and grew up in the Bengal region of India. He served in the Bengal army and came to Britain in 1782. He then moved to Ireland and eloped with an Irish girl called Jane Daly in 1786, returning to England at the turn of the century. In 1810 he opened the Hindoostane Coffee House in George Street, London. It was the first curry house to open in Britain. Mahomet and his wife also introduced 'shampooing', the Indian art of head massage, to Britain. ⊞

Find out more

Lancashire was the birthplace of the Industrial Revolution because it had fast flowing streams to drive the steam-powered machinery. In addition, coal was found in large quantities in Lancashire.

Check your learning

3.47 In which of the following industries did Richard Arkwright make great improvements?

☐ Coal ☐ Steel

☐ Textile ☐ Tobacco

🇬🇧 The slave trade

This commercial expansion and prosperity was <u>sustained</u> in part by the booming slave trade. While <u>slavery</u> was illegal within Britain itself, by the 18th century it was a fully established overseas industry, <u>dominated</u> by Britain and the American colonies.

Slaves came primarily from West Africa. Travelling on British ships in horrible conditions, they were taken to America and the Caribbean, where they were made to work on tobacco and sugar plantations. The living and working conditions for slaves were very bad. Many slaves tried to escape and others revolted against their owners in protest at their terrible treatment.

There were, however, people in Britain who opposed the slave trade. The first formal anti-slavery groups were set up by the Quakers in the late 1700s, and they petitioned Parliament to ban the practice. William Wilberforce, an <u>evangelical Christian</u> and a member of Parliament, also played an important

part in changing the law. Along with other abolitionists (people who supported the abolition of slavery), he succeeded in turning public opinion against the slave trade. In 1807, it became illegal to trade slaves in British ships or from British ports, and in 1833 the <u>Emancipation</u> Act abolished slavery throughout the British Empire. The Royal Navy stopped slave ships from other countries, freed the slaves and

Emblem used during the campaign to abolish slavery, 1788

punished the slave traders. After 1833, two million Indian and Chinese workers were employed to replace the freed slaves. They worked on sugar plantations in the Caribbean, in mines in South Africa, on railways in East Africa and in the army in Kenya.

Check your learning

3.48 Complete the following sentence:

People who wanted slavery to end are called _____.

3.49 The Emancipation Act ended slavery throughout the British Empire in:

☐ 1807 ☐ 1813
☐ 1833 ☐ 1840

The American War of Independence

By the 1760s, there were substantial British colonies in North America. The colonies were wealthy and largely in control of their own affairs. Many of the colonist families had originally gone to North America in order to have religious freedom. They were well educated and interested in ideas of liberty. The British government wanted to tax the colonies. The colonists saw this as an attack on their freedom and said there should be 'no taxation without representation' in the British Parliament. Parliament tried to compromise by repealing some of the taxes, but relationships between the British government and the colonies continued to worsen. Fighting broke out between the colonists and the British forces. In 1776, 13 American colonies declared their independence, stating that people had a right to establish their own governments. The colonists eventually defeated the British army and Britain recognised the colonies' independence in 1783.

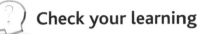 **Check your learning**

3.50 Which of the following sentences is correct?

  A People living in the American colonies wanted to be independent and have their own government.

  B People living in the American colonies wanted to be ruled by the British Parliament.

Find out more

The 'Boston Tea Party' was a political protest by the Sons of Liberty in Boston against British taxes. On 16 December 1773, after officials in Boston refused to return three shiploads of taxed tea to Britain, a group of colonists boarded the ships and destroyed the tea by throwing it into Boston Harbour.

US stamp depicting the Boston Tea Party

🇬🇧 War with France

During the 18th century, Britain fought a number of wars with France. In 1789, there was a revolution in France and the new French government soon declared war on Britain. Napoleon, who became Emperor of France, continued the war. Britain's navy fought against combined French and Spanish fleets, winning the Battle of Trafalgar in 1805. Admiral Nelson was in charge of the British fleet at Trafalgar and was killed in the battle. Nelson's Column in Trafalgar Square, London, is a monument to him. His ship, *HMS Victory*, can be visited in Portsmouth. The British army also fought against the French. In 1815, the French Wars ended with the defeat of the Emperor Napoleon by the Duke of Wellington at the Battle of Waterloo. Wellington was known as the Iron Duke and later became Prime Minister. 🇬🇧

Nelson's Column

🧠 Check your learning

3.51 Without looking at the text can you remember the dates of the following battles?

Battle of Trafalgar   _____

Battle of Waterloo   _____

The Union Flag

Although Ireland had had the same <u>monarch</u> as England and Wales since Henry VIII, it had remained a separate country. In 1801, Ireland became <u>unified</u> with England, Scotland and Wales after the Act of Union of 1800. This created the United Kingdom of Great Britain and Ireland. One symbol of this union between England, Scotland, Wales and Ireland was a new version of the official flag, the Union Flag. This is often called the Union Jack. The flag combined crosses associated with England, Scotland and Ireland. It is still used today as the official flag of the UK.

The Union Flag consists of three crosses:

- The cross of St George, patron saint of England, is a red cross on a white ground.
- The cross of St Andrew, patron saint of Scotland, is a diagonal white cross on a blue ground.
- The cross of St Patrick, patron saint of Ireland, is a diagonal red cross on a white ground.

There is also an official Welsh flag, which shows a Welsh dragon. The Welsh dragon does not appear on the Union Flag because, when the first Union Flag was created in 1606 from the flags of Scotland and England, the <u>Principality</u> of Wales was already united with England.

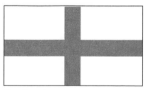

England

Scotland

Ireland

Wales

Check your learning

3.52 Can you match the countries with their patron saints?

A England   B Ireland   C Scotland

St Andrew   St George   St Patrick

Find out more

The patron saint of Wales is Saint David who was a Welsh bishop during the 6th century. Saint David's Day is on 1 March each year, the date he died. The date became a national day of celebration in Wales in the 18th century.

The Victorian Age

In 1837, Queen Victoria became queen of the UK at the age of 18. She reigned until 1901, almost 64 years. At the date of writing (2013) this is the longest reign of any British monarch. Her reign is known as the Victorian Age. It was a time when Britain increased in power and influence abroad. Within the UK, the middle classes became increasingly significant and a number of reformers led moves to improve conditions of life for the poor.

Statue of Queen Victoria

Check your learning

3.53 Without looking at the text, can you remember how long Victoria was Queen?

_____

🇬🇧 The British Empire

During the Victorian period, the British Empire grew to cover all of India, Australia and large parts of Africa. It became the largest empire the world has ever seen, with an estimated population of more than 400 million people.

Many people were encouraged to leave the UK to settle overseas. Between 1853 and 1913, as many as 13 million British citizens left the country. People continued to come to Britain from other parts of the world. For example, between 1870 and 1914, around 120,000 Russian and Polish Jews came to Britain to escape persecution. Many settled in London's East End and in Manchester and Leeds. People from the Empire, including India and Africa, also came to Britain to live, work and study. 🇬🇧

Check your learning

3.54 Without looking at the text, can you remember the number of people living in the British Empire at the time of Queen Victoria?

_____

3.55 How many people left the country between 1853 and 1914?

_____

Find out more

© Antonio Abrignani / Shutterstock.com

During Queen Victoria's reign, only Protestants could become Prime Minister. Her favourite Prime Minister, Benjamin Disraeli, was born of Jewish descent but was christened in the Church of England at the age of 12.

Benjamin Disraeli

🇬🇧 Trade and industry

Britain continued to be a great trading nation. The government began to promote policies of free trade, abolishing a number of taxes on imported goods. One example of this was the repealing of the Corn Laws in 1846. These had prevented the import of cheap grain. The reforms helped the development of British industry, because raw materials could now be imported more cheaply.

Working conditions in factories gradually became better. In 1847, the number of hours that women and children could work was limited by law to 10 hours per day. Better housing began to be built for workers.

Transport links also improved, enabling goods and people to move more easily around the country. Just before Victoria came to the throne, the father and son George and Robert Stephenson pioneered the railway engine and a major expansion of the railways took place in the Victorian period. Railways were built throughout the Empire. There were also great advances in other areas, such as the building of bridges by engineers such as Isambard Kingdom Brunel.

British industry led the world in the 19th century. The UK produced more than half of the world's iron, coal and cotton cloth. The UK also became a centre for financial services, including insurance and banking. In 1851, the Great Exhibition opened in Hyde Park in the Crystal Palace, a huge building made of steel and glass. Exhibits ranged from huge machines to handmade goods. Countries from all over the world showed their goods but most of the objects were made in Britain.

Isambard Kingdom Brunel (1806–59)

Brunel was originally from Portsmouth, England. He was an engineer who built tunnels, bridges, railway lines and ships. He was responsible for constructing the Great Western Railway, which was the first major railway built in Britain. It runs from Paddington Station in London to the south west of England, the West Midlands and Wales. Many of Brunel's bridges are still in use today. 🇬🇧

Check your learning

3.56 Is the following sentence **True** or **False**?

Free trade helped the development of British industry, because raw materials could be imported more cheaply.

3.57 Which **one** of the following did Isambard Kingdom Brunel design?

☐ The Great Western Railway   ☐ The Bessemer Converter

☐ The Crystal Palace   ☐ The first railway engine

⊞ The Crimean War

From 1853 to 1856, Britain fought with Turkey and France against Russia in the Crimean War. It was the first war to be extensively covered by the media through news stories and photographs. The conditions were very poor and many soldiers died from illnesses they caught in the hospitals, rather than from war wounds. Queen Victoria introduced the Victoria Cross medal during this war. It honours acts of valour by soldiers.

Florence Nightingale (1820–1910)

Florence Nightingale was born in Italy to English parents. At the age of 31, she trained as a nurse in Germany. In 1854, she went to Turkey and worked in military hospitals, treating soldiers who were fighting in the Crimean War. She and her fellow nurses improved the conditions in the hospital and reduced the mortality rate. In 1860 she established the Nightingale Training School for nurses at St Thomas' Hospital in London. The school was the first of its kind and still exists today, as do many of the practices that Florence used. She is often regarded as the founder of modern nursing. ⊞

Check your learning

3.58 Which of the following statements is correct?

A Because of Florence Nightingale and her fellow nurses, fewer wounded soldiers died in hospital during the Crimean War than in earlier wars.

B Because of Florence Nightingale and her fellow nurses, more wounded soldiers died in hospital during the Crimean War than in earlier wars.

Find out more

The first time the British public was able to read about the realities of war was during the Crimean War. The best known reporter was an Irishman, William Russell, who wrote for *The Times*. His reports encouraged Florence Nightingale to go out to the Crimea to care for wounded soldiers. He also wrote about Mary Seacole who, after the government refused to help her, travelled from Jamaica at her own expense to nurse British soldiers.

Ireland in the 19th century

Conditions in Ireland were not as good as in the rest of the UK. Two-thirds of the population still depended on farming to make their living, often on very small plots of land. Many depended on potatoes as a large part of their diet. In the middle of the century the potato crop failed, and Ireland suffered a famine. A million people died from disease and starvation. Another million and a half left Ireland. Some emigrated to the United States and others came to England. By 1861 there were large populations of Irish people in cities such as Liverpool, London, Manchester and Glasgow.

The Irish Nationalist movement had grown strongly through the 19th century. Some, such as the Fenians, favoured complete independence. Others, such as Charles Stuart Parnell, advocated 'Home Rule', in which Ireland would remain in the UK but have its own parliament.

Check your learning

3.59 How many people left Ireland during the potato famine?

☐ Half a million   ☐ A million and a half

☐ A million   ☐ Two million

🇬🇧 The right to vote

As the middle classes in the wealthy industrial towns and cities grew in influence, they began to demand more political power. The Reform Act of 1832 had greatly increased the number of people with the right to vote. The Act also abolished the old pocket and rotten boroughs (see page 81) and more parliamentary <u>seats</u> were given to the towns and cities. There was a permanent shift of political power from the countryside to the towns but voting was still based on ownership of property. This meant that members of the working class were still unable to vote.

A movement began to demand the vote for the working classes and other people without property. Campaigners, called the Chartists, presented petitions to Parliament. At first they seemed to be unsuccessful, but in 1867 there was another Reform Act. This created many more urban seats in Parliament and reduced the amount of property that people needed to have before they could vote. However, the majority of men still did not have the right to vote and no women could vote.

Politicians realised that the increased number of voters meant that they needed to persuade people to vote for them if they were to be sure of being elected to Parliament. The political parties began to create organisations to reach out to ordinary voters. Universal suffrage (the right of every adult, male or female, to vote) followed in the next century.

In common with the rest of Europe, women in 19th century Britain had fewer rights than men. Until 1870, when a woman got married, her earnings, property and money automatically belonged to her husband. Acts of

Parliament in 1870 and 1882 gave wives the right to keep their own earnings and property. In the late 19th and early 20th centuries, an increasing number of women campaigned and demonstrated for greater rights and, in particular, the right to vote. They formed the women's <u>suffrage</u> movement and became known as 'suffragettes'.

Find out more

Emmeline Pankhurst

Emmeline Pankhurst was leader of the British suffragette movement, which helped women win the right to vote. In 1999 *Time* magazine named Pankhurst as one of the 100 Most Important People of the 20th Century, stating: *'she shaped an idea of women for our time; she shook society into a new pattern from which there could be no going back'.*

Check your learning

3.60 Without looking at the text, can you name the law which gave the right to vote to more people?

⊞ The future of the Empire

Although the British Empire continued to grow until the 1920s, there was already discussion in the late 19th century about its future direction. Supporters of expansion believed that the Empire benefited Britain through increased trade and commerce. Others thought the Empire had become over-expanded and that the frequent conflicts in many parts of the Empire, such as India's north-west frontier or southern Africa, were a drain on resources. Yet the great majority of British people believed in the Empire as a force for good in the world.

The Boer War of 1899 to 1902 made the discussions about the future of the Empire more urgent. The British went to war in South Africa with settlers from the Netherlands called the Boers. The Boers fought fiercely and the war went on for over three years. Many died in the fighting and many more from disease. There was some public sympathy for the Boers and people began to question whether the Empire could continue. As different parts of the Empire developed, they won greater freedom and autonomy from Britain. Eventually, by the second half of the 20th century, there was, for the most part, an orderly transition from Empire to Commonwealth, with countries being granted their independence. ⊞

⊕ Check your learning

Complete the following sentence:

3.61 The British went to war in South Africa in 1899 with settlers called the

_____.

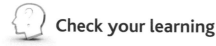 Rudyard Kipling (1865–1936)

Rudyard Kipling was born in India in 1865 and later lived in India, the UK and the USA. He wrote books and poems set in both India and the UK. His poems and novels reflected the idea that the British Empire was a force for good. Kipling was awarded the Nobel Prize in Literature in 1907. His books include the *Just So Stories* and *The Jungle Book*, which continue to be popular today. His poem *If* has often been voted among the UK's favourite poems. It begins with these words:

> '*If you can keep your head when all about you*
> *Are losing theirs and blaming it on you;*
> *If you can trust yourself when all men doubt you,*
> *But make allowance for their doubting too;*
> *If you can wait and not be tired by waiting,*
> *Or being lied about, don't deal in lies,*
> *Or being hated, don't give way to hating,*
> *And yet don't look too good, nor talk too wise*'
>
> (*If*, Rudyard Kipling)

 Check your learning

3.62 Without looking at the text, write down the name of one of Rudyard Kipling's books.

Study tip

When you come across a word, phrase or sentence you do not understand, write it down in a question. Then look it up. It is a good idea to keep a list of questions in your notes with the answers on a different page. Use the questions to help you with your revision.

Study tip

On the next page is a timeline to help you to remember the dates in this section. We have started it for you. Fill in the blank spaces and add your own notes. You can also add other key events in the country you came from that happened at the same time.

Key events in the UK	Periods and dates	Key events in the country you came from
1650–1800		
The ....of .... confirmed the rights of Parliament	1689	
Jewish refugees came to settle in Britain	1650s–1720	
Act or Treaty of Union signed between .... and .... creating the Kingdom of Great Britain	1707	
A German, ..., became king	....	
Sir Robert Walpole became the first P............. M..............	1721–1742	
Rebellion led by Bonnie Prince Charlie started	....	
Bonnie Prince Charlie defeated at the Battle of	....	
Beginning of the Industrial Revolution	Throughout the 18th century	
.... War of Independence	1776–1783	
French Revolution	....	
1800 onwards		
Admiral Nelson won the Battle of	1805	
Duke of .... defeated .... at the Battle of Waterloo	....	
.... was united with England, Scotland and Wales after the 1800 Act of Union and the Union Jack became our flag	1801	
The .... Act abolished rotten and pocket boroughs and gave more people the right to vote	....	
.... became queen at the age of 18	1837	

Key events in the UK	Periods and dates	Key events in the country you came from
1800 onwards (cont.)		
.... million British people left the UK to settle overseas	1870–1914	
Around 120,000 .... escaped to Britain from .... and Poland	1870–1914	
Parliament repealed .... Laws	1846	
Parliament pass a law to limit the working hours of women and children to .... hours a day	....	
The .... opened in Hyde Park in the .... Palace	....	
Britain, France and Turkey fought the .... War against Russia	.... to 1856	
A new Reform Act was passed	1867	
New laws gave women the right to keep their own earnings and property	1870 and	
The Boer War	1899 to	

Check your understanding – A global power

Now that you have read Section 4, what can you remember about the following?

- How Parliament became more powerful and the monarchy gave up some of its powers
- The Bill of Rights, 1689
- The beginnings of a free press
- The emigration of British people to the colonies and the arrival of refugees and other immigrants to Britain
- The events that led to Scotland joining England and Wales to become Great Britain
- The rebellion led by Bonnie Prince Charlie that began and ended in Scotland
- Some of the great thinkers of the Enlightenment and their ideas
- The Industrial Revolution and how it changed society
- The war against Napoleon in Europe
- The slave trade and how it ended
- The growth of the British Empire
- How democracy developed

SECTION 5 The 20th century

In this section you will read about the following:

- ◼ **improvements in society that led to better living conditions**
- ◼ **how British soldiers fought alongside their allies and soldiers from countries in the Empire in the First World War**
- ◼ **the partition of Ireland and the creation of the UK as it is today**
- ◼ **the world economic crisis called the Great Depression**
- ◼ **important events and people in the Second World War**

⊞ The First World War

The early 20th century was a time of <u>optimism</u> in Britain. The nation, with its expansive Empire, well-admired navy, thriving industry and strong political institutions, was what is now known as a global 'superpower'. It was also a time of social progress. Financial help for the unemployed, old-age pensions and free school meals were just a few of the important measures introduced. Various laws were passed to improve safety in the workplace; town planning rules were tightened to prevent the further development of <u>slums</u>; and better support was given to mothers and their children after divorce or separation. Local government became more democratic and a salary for members of Parliament (MPs) was introduced for the first time, making it easier for more people to take part in public life.

This era of optimism and progress was cut short when war broke out between several European nations. On 28 June 1914, Archduke Franz Ferdinand of Austria was assassinated. This set off a chain of events leading to the First World War (1914–18). But while the assassination provided the trigger for war, other factors – such as a growing sense of nationalism in many European states; increasing militarism; imperialism; and the division of the major European powers into two camps – all set the conditions for war.

The conflict was centred in Europe, but it was a global war involving nations from around the world. Britain was part of the Allied Powers, which included (amongst others) France, Russia, Japan, Belgium, Serbia – and later, Greece, Italy, Romania and the United States.

The whole of the British Empire was involved in the conflict – for example, more than a million Indians fought on behalf of Britain in lots of different countries, and around 40,000 were killed. Men from the West Indies, Africa, Australia, New Zealand and Canada also fought with the British. The Allies fought against the Central Powers – mainly Germany, the Austro-Hungarian Empire, the Ottoman Empire and later Bulgaria. Millions of people were killed or wounded, with more than two million British <u>casualties</u>. One battle, the British attack on the Somme in July 1916, resulted in about 60,000 British casualties on the first day alone.

The First World War ended at 11.00 am on 11th November 1918 with victory for Britain and its allies.

Americans
front line Trench,
France *First World War trench*

 **Check your learning**

3.63 Which two of the following did Parliament introduce in the early 20th century?

- ☐ Grants for university students
- ☐ Old age pensions
- ☐ Child benefit
- ☐ Free school meals

3.64 Without looking at the text, can you remember which country in the Empire sent more than a million soldiers to fight on Britain's side?

Find out more

The red poppy is used as a symbol for those who died in the First World War and later wars. It was adopted by the Royal British Legion as the symbol for their Poppy Appeal, to raise money to help those serving in the British Armed Forces.

© rosesmith / Shutterstock.com

Wreaths of poppies

🇬🇧 The partition of Ireland

In 1913, the British government promised 'Home Rule' for Ireland. The proposal was to have a self-governing Ireland with its own parliament but still part of the UK. A Home Rule Bill was introduced in Parliament. It was opposed by the Protestants in the north of Ireland, who threatened to resist Home Rule by force.

The outbreak of the First World War led the British government to postpone any changes in Ireland. Irish Nationalists were not willing to wait and in 1916 there was an uprising (the Easter Rising) against the British in Dublin. The leaders of the uprising were executed under military law. A guerrilla war against the British army and the police in Ireland followed. In 1921 a peace treaty was signed and in 1922 Ireland became two countries. The six counties in the north which were mainly Protestant remained part of the UK under the name Northern Ireland. The rest of Ireland became the Irish Free State. It had its own government and became a republic in 1949.

There were people in both parts of Ireland who disagreed with the split between the North and the South. They still wanted Ireland to be one independent country. Years of disagreement led to a terror campaign in Northern Ireland and elsewhere. The conflict between those wishing for full Irish independence and those wishing to remain loyal to the British government is often referred to as 'the Troubles'. 🇬🇧

Find out more

The Irish Republican Army (IRA), an Irish republican revolutionary military organisation, followed on from the Irish Volunteers, the organisation responsible for the Easter Rising. The IRA was the main group fighting for full Irish independence against the British government in Northern Ireland.

 Check your learning

3.65 Which of the following sentences is correct?

   A In 1922 Ireland became two independent countries called Northern Ireland and Southern Ireland.

   B In 1922 Ireland became two countries: the Irish Free State had its own government, and Northern Ireland remained part of the UK.

🇬🇧 The inter-war period

In the 1920s, many people's living conditions got better. There were improvements in public housing and new homes were built in many towns and cities. However, in 1929, the world entered the 'Great Depression' and some parts of the UK suffered mass unemployment. The effects of the depression of the 1930s were felt differently in different parts of the UK. The traditional heavy industries such as shipbuilding were badly affected but new industries – including the automobile and aviation industries – developed. As prices generally fell, those in work had more money to spend. Car ownership doubled from one million to two million between 1930 and 1939. In addition, many new houses were built. It was also a time of cultural <u>blossoming</u>, with writers such as Graham Greene and Evelyn Waugh prominent. The economist John Maynard Keynes published <u>influential</u> new theories of economics. The BBC started radio broadcasts in 1922 and began the world's first regular television service in 1936.

Check your learning

3.66 Match the following events with their dates:

A Start of the Great Depression   ☐ 1922
B First regular television service   ☐ 1929
C First BBC radio broadcasts   ☐ 1936

The Second World War

Adolf Hitler came to power in Germany in 1933. He believed that the conditions imposed on Germany by the Allies after the First World War were unfair; he also wanted to conquer more land for the German people. He set about renegotiating treaties, building up <u>arms</u>, and testing Germany's military strength in nearby countries. The British government tried to avoid another war. However, when Hitler invaded Poland in 1939, Britain and France declared war in order to stop his aggression.

The war was initially fought between the Axis powers (<u>fascist</u> Germany and Italy and the Empire of Japan) and the Allies. The main countries on the allied side were the UK, France, Poland, Australia, New Zealand, Canada, and the Union of South Africa.

Having occupied Austria and invaded Czechoslovakia, Hitler followed his invasion of Poland by taking control of Belgium and the Netherlands. Then, in 1940, German forces defeated allied troops and advanced through France. At this time of national crisis, Winston Churchill became Prime Minister and Britain's war leader.

Winston Churchill (1874–1965)

© Neftali / Shutterstock.com

Churchill was the son of a politician and, before becoming a Conservative MP in 1900, was a soldier and journalist. In May 1940 he became Prime Minister. He refused to surrender to the Nazis and was an inspirational leader to the British people in a time of great hardship. He lost the General Election in 1945 but returned as Prime Minister in 1951.

He was an MP until he stood down at the 1964 General Election. Following his death in 1965, he was given a state funeral. He remains a much-admired figure to this day, and in 2002 was voted the greatest Briton of all time by the public. During the War, he made many famous speeches including lines which you may still hear:

'I have nothing to offer but blood, toil, tears and sweat'

Churchill's first speech to the House of Commons after he became Prime Minister, 1940

'We shall fight on the beaches,
we shall fight on the landing grounds,
we shall fight in the fields and in the streets,
we shall fight in the hills;
we shall never surrender'

Speech to the House of Commons after Dunkirk (see page 112), 1940

'Never in the field of human conflict was so much owed by so many to so few'
Speech to the House of Commons during the Battle of Britain
(see below), 1940

As France fell, the British decided to <u>evacuate</u> British and French soldiers from France in a huge naval operation. Many civilian volunteers in small pleasure and fishing boats from Britain helped the Navy to rescue more than 300,000 men from the beaches around Dunkirk. Although many lives and a lot of equipment were lost, the evacuation was a success and meant that Britain was better able to continue the fight against the Germans. The evacuation gave rise to the phrase 'the Dunkirk spirit'.

From the end of June 1940 until the German invasion of the Soviet Union in June 1941, Britain and the Empire stood almost alone against Nazi Germany.

Hitler wanted to invade Britain, but before sending in troops, Germany needed to control the air. The Germans <u>waged</u> an air campaign against Britain, but the British resisted with their fighter planes and eventually won the <u>crucial aerial battle</u> against the Germans, called 'the Battle of Britain', in the summer of 1940. The most important planes used by the Royal Air Force in the Battle of Britain were the Spitfire and the Hurricane – which were designed and built in Britain. Despite this crucial victory, the German air force was able to continue bombing London and other British cities at night-time. This was called the Blitz. Coventry was almost totally destroyed and a great deal of damage was done in other cities, especially in the East End of London. Despite the destruction, there was a strong national spirit of resistance in the UK. The phrase 'the Blitz spirit' is still used today to describe Britons pulling together in the face of <u>adversity</u>.

At the same time as defending Britain, the British military was fighting the Axis on many other fronts. In Singapore, the Japanese defeated the British and then occupied Burma, threatening India. The United States entered the war when the Japanese bombed its naval base at Pearl Harbour in December 1941.

That same year, Hitler attempted the largest invasion in history by attacking the Soviet Union. It was a fierce conflict, with huge losses on both sides. German forces were <u>ultimately</u> repelled by the <u>Soviets</u>, and the damage they sustained proved to be a <u>pivotal</u> point in the war.

The allied forces gradually <u>gained the upper hand</u>, winning significant victories in North Africa and Italy. German losses in the Soviet Union, combined with the support of the Americans, meant that the Allies were eventually strong enough to attack Hitler's forces in Western Europe. On 6 June 1944, allied forces landed in Normandy (this event is often referred to as 'D-Day'). Following victory on the beaches of Normandy, the allied forces pressed on through France and eventually into Germany. The Allies <u>comprehensively</u> defeated Germany in May 1945.

The war against Japan ended in August 1945 when the United States dropped its newly developed atom bombs on the Japanese cities of Hiroshima and Nagasaki. Scientists led by Ernest Rutherford, working at Manchester and then Cambridge University, were the first to 'split the atom' and took part in the Manhattan Project in the United States, which developed the atomic bomb. The war was finally over.

Alexander Fleming (1881–1955)

Born in Scotland, Fleming moved to London as a teenager and later qualified as a doctor. He was researching influenza (the 'flu') in 1928 when he discovered penicillin. This was then further developed into a usable drug by the scientists Howard Florey and Ernst Chain. By the 1940s it was in <u>mass production</u>. Fleming won the Nobel Prize in Medicine in 1945. Penicillin is still used to treat bacterial infections today. 🇬🇧

Check your learning

3.67 From where did the British navy rescue soldiers fleeing from Hitler's army with the help of volunteers in fishing and pleasure boats?

☐ Paris, France   ☐ Gdansk, Poland

☐ Dunkirk, France   ☐ Hamburg, Germany

3.68 Complete the following sentence:

The Spitfire and the Hurricane were the most important planes in the Battle of _____.

Study tip

Create your own timeline for Section 5

Key events in the UK	Periods and dates	Key events in a country you know well

Check your understanding – The 20th century

Now that you have read Section 5, what can you remember about the following?

- ■ The growth of Britain's wealth and power

- ■ Improvements in living and working conditions

- ■ Salaries for members of parliament and great local democracy

- ■ The First World War and how British soldiers fought alongside soldiers from the colonies and other countries as part of the Allied Powers

- ■ The partition of Ireland

- ■ The creation of Northern Ireland and the United Kingdom as it is today

- ■ How a period of prosperity ended with a world economic crisis called the Great Depression

- ■ Important events and people in the Second World War

SECTION 6 Britain since 1945

In this section you will read about the following:

■ **the establishment of the welfare state**

■ **how life in Britain changed in the 1960s and 1970s**

■ **British inventions of the 20th century**

■ **events since 1979**

The welfare state

Although the UK had won the war, the country was exhausted economically and the people wanted change. During the war, there had been significant reforms to the education system and people now looked for wider social reforms.

In 1945 the British people elected a Labour government. The new Prime Minister was Clement Attlee, who promised to introduce the welfare state outlined in the Beveridge Report. In 1948, Aneurin (Nye) Bevan, the Minister for Health, led the establishment of the National Health Service (NHS), which guaranteed a minimum standard of health care for all, free at the point of use. A national system of benefits was also introduced to provide 'social security', so that the population would be protected from the 'cradle to the grave'. The government took into public ownership (<u>nationalised</u>) the railways, coal mines and gas, water and electricity supplies.

Another aspect of change was self-government for former colonies. In 1947, independence was granted to nine countries, including India, Pakistan and Ceylon (now Sri Lanka). Other colonies in Africa, the Caribbean and the Pacific achieved independence over the next 20 years.

The UK developed its own atomic bomb and joined the new North Atlantic Treaty Organization (NATO), an <u>alliance</u> of nations set up to resist the <u>perceived threat</u> of invasion by the Soviet Union and its allies.

Britain had a Conservative government from 1951 to 1964. The 1950s were a period of economic recovery after the war and increasing prosperity for working people. The Prime Minister of the day, Harold Macmillan, was famous for his 'wind of change' speech about decolonisation and independence for the countries of the Empire.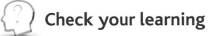

Check your learning

3.69 What was the name of the Prime Minister whose government created the National Health Service?

☐ Nye Bevan   ☐ Harold Macmillan

☐ Clement Attlee   ☐ Winston Churchill

3.70 Without looking at the text, can you name two colonies that became independent countries after 1947?

1. _____   2. _____

Clement Attlee (1883–1967)

Clement Attlee was born in London in 1883. His father was a solicitor and, after studying at Oxford University, Attlee became a barrister. He gave this up to do social work in East London and eventually became a Labour MP. He was Winston Churchill's Deputy Prime Minister in the wartime coalition government and became Prime Minister after the Labour Party won the 1945 election. He was Prime Minister from 1945 to 1951 and led the Labour Party for 20 years. Attlee's government <u>undertook</u> the nationalisation of major industries (like coal and steel), created the National Health Service and implemented many of Beveridge's plans for a stronger welfare state. Attlee also introduced measures to improve the conditions of workers.

William Beveridge (1879–1963)

William Beveridge (later Lord Beveridge) was a British economist and social reformer. He served briefly as a Liberal MP and was subsequently the leader of the Liberals in the House of Lords but is best known for the 1942 report *Social Insurance and Allied Services* (known as the Beveridge Report). The report was commissioned by the wartime government in 1941. It recommended that the government should find ways of fighting the five 'Giant Evils' of Want, Disease, Ignorance, <u>Squalor</u> and Idleness and provided the basis of the modern welfare state.

R A Butler (1902–82)

Richard Austen Butler (later Lord Butler) was born in 1902. He became a Conservative MP in 1923 and held several positions before becoming responsible for education in 1941. In this role, he oversaw the introduction of the Education Act 1944 (often called 'The Butler Act'), which introduced free secondary education in England and Wales. The education system has changed significantly since the Act was introduced, but the division between primary and secondary schools that it enforced still remains in most areas of Britain.

Dylan Thomas (1914–53)

Dylan Thomas was a Welsh poet and writer. He often read and performed his work in public, including for the BBC. His most well-known works include the radio play *Under Milk Wood*, first performed after his death in 1954, and the poem *Do Not Go Gentle into That Good Night*, which he wrote for his dying father in 1952. He died at the age of 39 in New York. There are several memorials to him in his birthplace, Swansea, including a statue and the Dylan Thomas Centre. 🇬🇧

Check your learning

3.71 On the next page we have listed some of the great improvements introduced by the government in the 1940s. Without looking at the text, can you write who did what? We have done one for you.

Who did what?

Clement Attlee   William Butler   Richard A Butler   Nye Bevan

	The Education Act 1944 Free secondary education in England and Wales
	Wrote the report that led to the creation of the welfare state
	Led the government that nationalised the railways, coal mines and gas, electricity and water supplies
Nye Bevan	Led the establishment of the National Health Service

Migration in post-war Britain

Rebuilding Britain after the Second World War was a huge task. There were labour shortages and the British government encouraged workers from Ireland and other parts of Europe to come to the UK and help with the reconstruction. In 1948, people from the West Indies were also invited to come and work.

During the 1950s, there was still a shortage of labour in the UK. Further immigration was therefore encouraged for economic reasons, and many industries advertised for workers from overseas. For example, centres were set up in the West Indies to recruit people to drive buses. Textile and engineering firms from the north of England and the Midlands sent agents to India and Pakistan to find workers. For about 25 years, people from the West Indies, India, Pakistan and (later) Bangladesh travelled to work and settle in Britain.

Check your learning

3.72 Is the following statement **True** or **False**?

After the Second World War, the government encouraged workers from Ireland and other parts of Europe to come to the UK to help rebuild Britain.

3.73 Complete the following sentences:

During the 1950s, centres were set up in the _____ _____ to recruit people to drive buses.

_____ and engineering firms from the north of England and the Midlands sent agents to _____ and _____ to find workers.

🇬🇧 Social change in the 1960s

The decade of the 1960s was a period of significant social change. It was known as 'the Swinging Sixties'. There was growth in British fashion, cinema and popular music. Two well-known pop music groups at the time were The Beatles and The Rolling Stones. People started to become <u>better off</u> and many bought cars and other <u>consumer goods</u>.

Statue of the Beatles

It was also a time when social laws were <u>liberalised</u>, for example in relation to divorce and to abortion in England, Wales and Scotland. The position of women in the workplace also improved. It was quite common at the time for employers to ask women to leave their jobs when they got married, but Parliament passed new laws giving women the right to equal pay and made it illegal for employers to discriminate against women because of their gender.

The 1960s was also a time of technological progress. Britain and France developed the world's only <u>supersonic</u> commercial airliner, Concorde. New styles of architecture, including high-rise buildings and the use of concrete and steel, became common.

The number of people migrating from the West Indies, India, Pakistan and what is now Bangladesh fell in the late 1960s because the government passed new laws to restrict immigration to Britain. Immigrants were required to have a strong connection to Britain through birth or ancestry. Even so, during the early 1970s, Britain admitted 28,000 people of Indian origin who had been forced to leave Uganda.

Check your learning

3.74 Which of the following statements is correct?

    A New laws in the 1960s made it easier to get an abortion or a divorce in England, Scotland and Wales.

    B New laws in the 1960s made it more difficult to get an abortion or a divorce in England, Scotland and Wales.

⊞ Some great British inventions of the 20th century

Britain has given the world some wonderful inventions. Examples from the 20th century include:

The television was developed by Scotsman John Logie Baird (1888–1946) in the 1920s. In 1932 he made the first television broadcast between London and Glasgow.

Radar was developed by Scotsman Sir Robert Watson-Watt (1892–1973), who proposed that enemy aircraft could be <u>detected</u> by radio waves. The first successful radar test took place in 1935.

Working with radar led Sir Bernard Lovell (1913–2012) to make new discoveries in astronomy. The radio telescope he built at Jodrell Bank in Cheshire was for many years the biggest in the world and continues to operate today.

A Turing machine is a <u>theoretical mathematical device</u> invented by Alan Turing (1912–54), a British mathematician, in the 1930s. The theory was influential in the development of computer science and the modern-day computer.

The Scottish <u>physician</u> and researcher John Macleod (1876–1935) was the co-discoverer of insulin, used to treat diabetes.

The structure of the DNA molecule was discovered in 1953 through work at British universities in London and Cambridge. This discovery contributed to many scientific advances, particularly in medicine and fighting crime. Francis Crick (1916–2004), one of those awarded the Nobel Prize for this discovery, was British.

The jet engine was developed in Britain in the 1930s by Sir Frank Whittle (1907–96), a British Royal Air Force engineer officer.

Sir Christopher Cockerell (1910–99), a British inventor, invented the hovercraft in the 1950s.

Britain and France developed Concorde, the world's only supersonic passenger aircraft. It first flew in 1969 and began carrying passengers in 1976. Concorde was retired from service in 2003.

The Harrier jump jet, an aircraft capable of taking off vertically, was also designed and developed in the UK.

In the 1960s, James Goodfellow (1937–) invented the cash-dispensing ATM (automatic teller machine) or 'cashpoint'. The first of these was put into use by Barclays Bank in Enfield, north London in 1967.

IVF (in-vitro fertilisation) therapy for the treatment of infertility was pioneered in Britain by physiologist Sir Robert Edwards (1925–) and gynaecologist Patrick Steptoe (1913–88). The world's first 'test-tube baby' was born in Oldham, Lancashire in 1978.

© Jason Benz Bennee / Shutterstock.com

In 1996, two British scientists, Sir Ian Wilmut (1944–) and Keith Campbell (1954–2012), led a team which was the first to succeed in cloning a mammal, Dolly the sheep. This has led to further research into the possible use of cloning to preserve endangered species and for medical purposes.

Sir Peter Mansfield (1933–), a British scientist, is the co-inventor of the MRI (magnetic resonance imaging) scanner. This enables doctors and researchers to obtain exact and non-invasive images of human internal organs and has revolutionised diagnostic medicine.

The inventor of the World Wide Web, Sir Tim Berners-Lee (1955–), is British. Information was successfully transferred via the web for the first time on 25 December 1990.

i NOTE

Remember that you do not have to learn the dates of birth and death of the people mentioned in the text.

Check your learning

3.75 There is a lot of information to remember in this section. Try using some of the study tips in Chapter 1 to learn who invented or discovered what, then complete the table below. We have filled in some of it to help you.

Inventor	Famous for
Technology and electronics	
John Logie Baird	
Sir Robert Watson-Watt	Radar
	Astronomy, Jodrell Bank
Alan Turing	
	Jet engine
Sir Peter Mansfield	MRI (magnetic resonance imaging) scanner
	World Wide Web
Biology and medicine	
	Discovering insulin
Francis Crick	
Sir Robert Edwards and Patrick Steptoe	In-vitro fertilisation (IVF)
James Goodfellow	
Sir Ian Wilmott and Keith Campbell	

Study tip

To help you remember the information on British inventions, we have drawn a spider diagram below. You could copy it on a large piece of paper and add pictures to make it even more memorable.

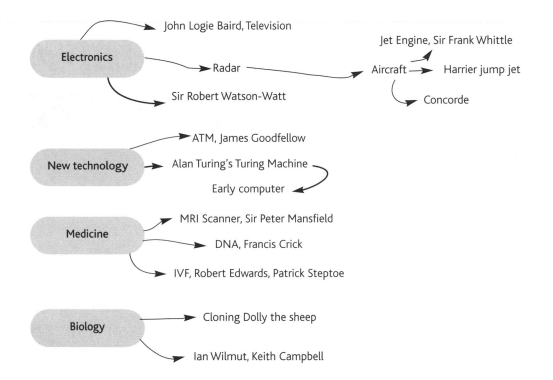

Problems in the economy in the 1970s

In the late 1970s, the post-war <u>economic boom</u> came to an end. Prices of goods and raw materials began to rise sharply and the exchange rate between the pound and other currencies was unstable. This caused problems with the 'balance of payments': imports of goods were valued at more than the price paid for exports.

Many industries and services were affected by <u>strikes</u> and this caused problems between the trade unions and the <u>government</u>. People began to argue that the unions were too powerful and that their activities were harming the UK.

The 1970s were also a time of serious <u>unrest</u> in Northern Ireland. In 1972, the Northern Ireland Parliament was suspended and Northern Ireland was directly ruled by the UK government. Some 3,000 people lost their lives in the decades after 1969 in the violence in Northern Ireland.

Mary Peters (1939–)

Born in Manchester, Mary Peters moved to Northern Ireland as a child. She was a talented athlete who won an Olympic gold medal in the pentathlon in 1972. After this, she raised money for local athletics and became the team manager for the women's British Olympic team. She continues to promote sport and tourism in Northern Ireland and was made a Dame of the British Empire in 2000 in recognition of her work.

 **Check your learning**

3.76 Is the sentence below **True** or **False**?

Britain had a problem with the 'balance of payments' in the 1970s because the country earned less for the goods it sold than the goods it bought from other countries.

British goods sold to other countries   Goods bought from other countries

⊞ Europe and the Common Market

West Germany, France, Belgium, Italy, Luxembourg and the Netherlands formed the European Economic Community (EEC) in 1957. At first the UK did not wish to join the EEC but it eventually did so in 1973. The UK is a full member of the European Union but does not use the Euro currency. ⊞

Check your learning

3.77 Complete the following sentence:

The UK joined the European Economic Community (EEC) in

_____ .

⊞ Conservative government from 1979 to 1997

Margaret Thatcher, Britain's first woman Prime Minister, led the Conservative government from 1979 to 1990. The government made structural changes to the economy through the privatisation of nationalised industries and imposed legal controls on trade union powers.

Deregulation saw a great increase in the role of the City of London as an international centre for investments, insurance and other financial services. Traditional industries, such as shipbuilding and coal mining, declined. In 1982, Argentina invaded the Falkland Islands, a British overseas territory in the South Atlantic. A naval taskforce was sent from the UK and military action led to the recovery of the islands.

John Major was Prime Minister after Mrs Thatcher, and helped establish the Northern Ireland peace process.

Margaret Thatcher (1925–)

Margaret Thatcher was the daughter of a grocer from Grantham in Lincolnshire. She trained as a chemist and lawyer. She was elected as a Conservative MP in 1959 and became a cabinet minister in 1970 as the

Secretary of State for Education and Science. In 1975 she was elected as Leader of the Conservative Party and so became Leader of the Opposition.

Following the Conservative victory in the General Election in 1979, Margaret Thatcher became the first woman Prime Minister of the UK. She was the longest-serving Prime Minister of the 20th century, remaining in office until 1990.

During her premiership, there were a number of important economic reforms within the UK. She worked closely with the United States President, Ronald Reagan, and was one of the first Western leaders to recognise and welcome the changes in the leadership of the Soviet Union, which eventually led to the end of the Cold War.

Check your learning

3.78 Which two of the following did Margaret Thatcher's government do?

☐ Sold the nationalised industries　　☐ Started the peace process in Northern Ireland

☐ Fought a war with Argentina　　☐ Ended the Cold War

🏴 Roald Dahl (1916–90)

Roald Dahl was born in Wales to Norwegian parents. He served in the Royal Air Force during the Second World War. It was during the 1940s that he began to publish books and short stories. He is most well known for his children's books, although he also wrote for adults. His best-known works include *Charlie and the Chocolate Factory* and *George's Marvellous Medicine*. Several of his books have been made into films.

Labour government from 1997 to 2010

In 1997 the Labour Party led by Tony Blair was elected. The Blair government introduced a Scottish Parliament and a Welsh Assembly (see pages 237–238). The Scottish Parliament has substantial powers to <u>legislate</u>. The Welsh Assembly was given fewer <u>legislative powers</u> but considerable control over public services. In Northern Ireland, the Blair government was able to build on the peace process, resulting in the Good Friday Agreement signed in 1998. The Northern Ireland Assembly was elected in 1999 but suspended in 2002. It was not reinstated until 2007. Most paramilitary groups in Northern Ireland have <u>decommissioned</u> their arms and are inactive. Gordon Brown took over as Prime Minister in 2007. 🏴

© David Fowler / Shutterstock.com

Tony Blair and Gordon Brown

Check your learning

3.79 Is the following sentence **True** or **False?**

The Blair government introduced a Scottish Parliament and Welsh Assembly but did not allow Northern Ireland any form of government.

Find out more

The Northern Ireland peace process and the Good Friday Agreement

The British government had secret meetings with the Irish nationalist parties that wanted to be part of the Republic of Ireland, including groups that used violence, such as the Irish Republican Army (IRA). The Irish government and the loyalist groups that wanted to remain in the United Kingdom were also consulted. These negotiations took place over many years. Finally, on Good Friday 1998, all the parties involved signed a peace agreement. Now the loyalists and nationalists work together as members of Northern Ireland's National Assembly.

Conflicts in Afghanistan and Iraq

Throughout the 1990s, Britain played a leading role in coalition forces involved in the liberation of Kuwait, following the Iraqi invasion in 1990, and the conflict in the Former Republic of Yugoslavia. Since 2000, British armed forces have been engaged in the global fight against international terrorism and against the proliferation of weapons of mass destruction, including operations in Afghanistan and Iraq. British combat troops left Iraq in 2009. The UK now operates in Afghanistan as part of the United Nations (UN) mandated 50-nation International Security Assistance Force (ISAF) coalition and at the invitation of the Afghan government. ISAF is working to ensure that Afghan territory can never again be used as a safe haven for international terrorism, where groups such as Al Qa'ida could plan attacks on the international community. As part of this, ISAF is building up the Afghan

National Security Forces and is helping to create a secure environment in which governance and development can be extended. International forces are gradually handing over responsibility for security to the Afghans, who will have full security responsibility in all provinces by the end of 2014. 🇬🇧

Check your learning

3.80 Without looking at the text, can you name two countries where the British armed forces have been fighting since the 1990s?

1._____ 2. _____

🇬🇧 Coalition government 2010 onwards

In May 2010, and for the first time in the UK since February 1974, no political party won an overall majority in the General Election. The Conservative and Liberal Democrat parties formed a coalition and the leader of the Conservative Party, David Cameron, became Prime Minister. 🇬🇧

Check your learning:

3.81 Complete the following sentence:

After the General Election in May 2010 the Conservatives and Liberal Democrat parties formed a _____ government.

Check your understanding – Britain since 1945

Now that you have read Section 6, what can you remember about the following?

- The establishment of the welfare state and the people responsible for creating it
- The nationalisation of the railways, mining and other industries and services
- How people were recruited from Ireland, India, Pakistan and the West Indies to work in Britain in the 1950s
- Social change and technological progress in the 1960s
- Great inventions of the 20th century
- How the government passed laws to restrict immigration from some countries in the 1960s
- Economic problems in the 1970s
- Violent unrest in Northern Ireland in the 1970s
- Britain joining the European Economic Community (EEC)
- The government of Margaret Thatcher, Britain's first woman Prime Minister and leader of the Conservative Party
- The privatisation of nationalised industries, the introduction of legal controls on trade union powers and the war with Argentina during Margaret Thatcher's government
- The beginning of the Northern Ireland peace process during the government of John Major, the Prime Minister after Margaret Thatcher
- The Labour government and the creation of the Scottish Parliament, the Northern Ireland and Welsh Assemblies
- Britain's involvement alongside international armed forces in Kuwait, the former Republic of Yugoslavia, Iraq and Afghanistan
- The Conservative and Liberal Democratic parties' coalition government led by Prime Minister David Cameron

Revision questions and end of chapter checklist

You have completed Chapter Three. Now that you have read the study materials, checked your learning and done a few tasks, try to answer the following revision questions. If you are not sure of the answers, use your notes or look back at the study material before checking the answers at the end of the chapter.

1   Where is the best preserved prehistoric village built in the Stone Age?

    Answer:
    _____

2   What was the name of the queen of the Iceni who fought against the Romans?

    Answer:
    _____

3   Who invaded Britain in 1066?

    Answer:
    _____

4   Who defeated the English army at the Battle of Bannockburn in 1314?

    Answer:
    _____

5   What were the owners of land in Ireland and the north of Scotland called?

    Answer:
    _____

6   When did King John and his noblemen sign the Magna Carta?

Answer:

7   Name one of the first books printed in English around 1400.

Answer:

8   Who won the Battle of Bosworth field and became the first Tudor king?

Answer:

9   Why did the Irish rebel against Elizabeth I and James I?

Answer:

10 Why did the Scots go to war with Cromwell?

Answer:

11 What was the name of the organisation formed to promote 'natural knowledge' during Charles II's reign?

Answer:

12 Who was Sir Robert Walpole?

Answer:

13 Who is known in Scotland as 'The Bard'?

Answer:

14 Why did people move from the countryside in the 18th century?

Answer:

15 What is the name of the document that limited the power of the monarch and increased that of Parliament in 1689?

Answer:

16 What did William Wilberforce work to abolish in the late 1700s?

Answer:

17 With which country did Britain fight a number of wars from 1789 to 1815?

Answer:

18 What did the Act of Union create in 1800?

Answer:

19 Name three people who improved transport links at the time of Queen Victoria.

Answer:

20 Which crop failed and caused a famine in Ireland in the middle of the 19th century?

Answer:

21 Name one thing the Chartists wanted.

Answer:

22 What did Rudyard Kipling win in 1907?

Answer:

23 Before which war did the government introduce a salary for MPs?

Answer:

24 What event made Britain and France decide to go to war with Hitler?

Answer:
_____

25 Who was born in Swansea, Wales and wrote *Under Milk Wood* and *Do Not Go Gentle into That Good Night*?

Answer:
_____

26 Name one of the pop groups of the 1960s.

Answer:
_____

27 What changed for women in the workplace in the 1960s?

Answer:
_____

28 When did the post-war economic boom end?

Answer:
_____

29 Who was Prime Minister when the Good Friday Agreement was signed in 1998?

Answer:
_____

30 Which two parties formed a coalition in 2010?

Answer:
_____

End of Chapter Three checklist

Now that you have come to the end of Chapter Three, tick the boxes when you have:

■ read the study material   ☐

■ made short notes, drawings and timelines to help you with your revision   ☐

■ looked up words that you don't understand and made a note of them   ☐

■ completed the 'Check your learning' and revision questions and
  checked your answers   ☐

■ read the study material again for the questions you got wrong   ☐

Glossary

abolished	Got rid off.
accomplished	(here) Skilled.
AD	Anno Domini – the years after Jesus Christ was born, when the modern Western calendar started. Also called the Christian Era (CE).
adversity	A very difficult situation.
advocated	To express support for a particular idea or way of doing things.
alliance	Group of countries that agree to work together.
allies	Friends or partners.
ancestor	A relative from many years ago.
annexed	To take over an area or country next to your own.
Archbishop	A very senior position in the Church of England and Catholic Church.
armed forces	The army, navy and air force which defend a country.
arms	Weapons such as guns or bombs.

BC	Before Christ – the years before Jesus Christ was born, also called Before the Christian Era (BCE).
Bessemer process	Process for making steel from iron.
better off	Richer, have more money.
bishop	A senior member of the clergy in the Catholic church and Church of England, often in charge of churches in a particular area.
blossom	Develop and become successful.
bonnie	Good looking, young and healthy.
cabinet	A group of senior ministers who are responsible for controlling government policy.
casualties	People wounded or killed in a war or accident.
centralising power	Taking control away from local places and ruling from a central government.
charter (government)	An official written statement that describes the rights and responsibilities of a state (or king) and its citizens.
chieftain	The leader of a clan in Scotland or Ireland.
civil war	War between groups of people who live in the same country.
clan	A group of people or families who are led by a chieftain and may be related to each other – a term used traditionally in Scotland.
clansmen	Male members of a clan.
clergy	Religious leaders, here used to describe Christian religious leaders.
coalition	Two or more groups, such as political parties, or countries joining together.
colonise	To take over and settle in another country. People who colonise are called colonists.

commemorate	To do something to show you remember an important person or event in the past.
comprehensively	Totally and completely.
conquered	Beaten in battle.
constituency	An area and the voters who live in it who elect an MP to represent them in Parliament.
constitutional monarchy	Type of government where the monarch is the head of state but has to follow the constitution.
consumer goods	Things that people buy to use.
controversial	A topic that causes a lot of argument.
crucial aerial battle	An important battle between air forces which made a difference in the war.
decommission	To take equipment or weapons out of use.
depression	Collapse of the economy with high levels of unemployment and businesses losing money.
deregulation	Removal of government rules.
detect	To discover or notice something, especially something that is difficult to see, hear or smell.
devout	Very religious.
Divine Right of Kings	The belief that a king's right to rule comes from God and that he does not have to listen to the people, nobles or parliament.
doctrine	A set of beliefs shared or taught by a religious group.
dominate	To be the most important part of something, to have the most power or influence.
dramatised	Made into a play or drama.
dynasty	A family that holds power for many years and passes it on to its children and relatives.
economic boom	Period when prices go up, wages rise and there is

	plenty of money in the economy.
emancipation	To give freedom or rights.
enlightenment	A period of progress in science, philosophy, arts and culture when traditional ideas were challenged and free thinking encouraged.
established official church	A church that is recognised by law as the official church of a state.
evacuate	To move people from a dangerous place to a safe one.
evangelical Christian	One who believes that faith in Jesus Christ and studying the Bible are more important than religious ceremonies.
executed	Killed as a punishment.
Fascist	Very right wing, nationalist and racist; for example, followers of Hitler and Mussolini.
found	(here) To start or set up.
gained the upper hand	Started winning.
General Election	An event when everyone who has the right to vote in a country chooses the people they want to represent them in their government.
gravity	The force that makes objects fall to the ground.
heir	Someone who will receive a person's money or possessions after they die.
house	(here) A family or dynasty (for example, the House of York).
House of Commons	The part of the UK Parliament where MPs who are elected by voters debate political issues.
hunter-gatherers	People who live by hunting for meat and collecting vegetables and fruit.
illegal	Something the law does not allow.

influential	Having a strong effect on how something or someone develops or behaves.
initially	At the beginning.
institution	(here) A large and important organisation.
invade	When an army enters another country by force.
legal	Allowed to do something by law.
legislate	Make laws.
legislative power	The power to make laws.
legitimate children	Children born to people who are married.
liberalise	Make laws and systems less strict.
liberty	Freedom.
Lord Lieutenant	The representative of the monarch in a particular area.
mandated	Gave official permission.
mass production	Produce a lot of goods cheaply using machines.
mechanised	The use of machines to do what used to be done by hand.
mint	To make coins with a stamp or mark on them, such as a king's face, to show they are official.
missionaries	Religious people who go to new places to spread their religion.
monarch	King or queen.
monastery	A place where men called monks live as a religious group.
monument	A building that is important in history; a structure built to remember an event or person.
mortality	Death.
nationalised	Bought and then controlled by central government – as in the case of an industry or service that was previously owned privately.

naval taskforce	A group of navy ships with a specific task to do.
nobility	Aristocracy; people who belong to the highest social class, some of whom have titles such as Lord, Duke, Earl or Baron, and who owned most of the land.
noblemen	Men from the nobility.
office, to be in	To be in power in government.
optimism	Belief that good things will happen.
party politics	The shared ideas and beliefs by an organised group of people.
patron saint	A Christian holy person believed to help and protect a particular place or group of people.
peasant	Poor person who works on the land growing crops or keeping animals.
perceived threat	Feeling that someone is going to do something bad to you.
physician	Doctor.
pilgrimage	A journey to a holy place.
pivotal	Very important.
plague	Serious disease that spreads quickly and kills lots of people.
Pope	Leader of the Roman Catholic Church.
postpone	Arrange for something to happen at a later time.
predominantly	Mainly.
preserved	In quite good condition, not too damaged.
Prime Minister	The politician who leads the government.
principality	A country with a prince as its head of state.
proclaim	To announce something officially or in public.
proliferation	A very quick increase in number.
prominent	Important.

Protestants	Christians who are not members of the Roman Catholic Church.
raid	Attack to rob from people.
Reformation	The religious movement in the 16th century that challenged the authority of the Pope and established Protestant churches in Europe.
refugee	A person who has to leave the country where they live, often because of war or persecution.
repeal	To end a law.
representation	Having someone to speak for a group of people.
resistance	Fighting back.
seat (Parliament)	A constituency.
serf	Poor people who worked on the land and were the property of the land owner.
shrine	A special place connected with a holy person or event where religious people go to pray.
slavery	A system in which people buy and sell other people who are forced to work without pay.
slum	A poor and crowded area where buildings are in a very bad condition.
sonnet	A poem that is 14 lines long and rhymes in a particular way.
sophisticated	Well-developed.
Soviets	States of the former USSR, led by Russia.
squalor	Very dirty and unpleasant conditions.
strike, to go on	Refuse to work in order to protest about something.
subject to	Has to obey.
submitting	Giving in.
succeed	(here) To become king or queen after the previous one dies.

successor	A person who takes over an office or receives some kind of power from another person – for example, the son who becomes king when his father dies is his successor.
suffrage	The right to vote in an election.
supersonic	Faster than the speed of sound.
sustain	Allow something to continue for a period of time.
terrorism	Violence and fear used by people who want to force a government to do something. The violence is usually random and unexpected, so that no one can feel safe.
theoretical mathematical device	A type of computer.
thrifty	Careful with money.
tomb	Place where a dead person is buried; may be built of stone or earth.
trade union	An organisation of workers formed to protect its members.
treaty	An official written agreement between countries or governments.
ultimately	Finally, after a series of things have happened.
undertake	To work on something.
unify	Join together two or more countries or groups to make a single one.
unrest	When people start making trouble because they are angry with the government.
uprising	A violent revolt or rebellion against an authority.
waged	(here) Carry out.

Answers to 'Check your learning' questions

Section 1 Early Britain

3.1   about 10,000 years ago
About 6,000 years ago

3.2   True

3.3

Skara Brae	Stonehenge	Maiden Castle
Orkney, Scotland	Wiltshire, England	Dorset, England
Stone Age	Stone Age	Iron Age

3.4   B Julius Caesar tried to invade Britain in 55 BC but failed.

3.5   St Augustine

3.6   B Scottish

3.7   A True
B False

Section 2 The Middle Ages

3.8   A True
B False

3.9   Henry V

3.10   ✓ England ✓ North of Scotland

3.11   The Magna Carta contains a list of rights that <u>King John</u> gave to his noblemen in the year <u>1215</u>.

3.12   By 1400 <u>English</u> replaced Norman French in Parliament and the royal court in England.

3.13   ✓ Scots

3.14 ✓ 1485

3.15 ✓ House of Lancaster ✓ House of York

Section 3 The Tudors and Stuarts

3.16 ✓ Henry VIII (Henry the Eighth)

3.17 Catherine of Aragon was the mother of <u>Mary I</u>
Anne Boleyn was the mother of <u>Elizabeth I</u>
Jane Seymour was the mother of <u>Edward VI</u>

3.18 ✓ 1560

3.19 ✓ cousin

3.20 A True
B False

3.21 *A Midsummer Night's Dream, Hamlet, Macbeth* or *Romeo and Juliet*

3.22 ✓ London

3.23 False Scotland remained a separate country with its own parliament
3.24 ✓ Henry VIII

3.25 The English government encouraged Scottish and English <u>Protestants</u> to settle in Ulster, the northern province of Ireland. These settlements were called <u>plantations</u>.

3.26 James I and Charles I believed that they were chosen by <u>God</u> to rule.

3.27 ✓ 1642

3.28 A The Puritans who opposed King Charles were a group of Protestants

3.29 A Battle of Marston Moor or Naseby
B Battle of Dunbar or Worcester

3.30 Parliament, Charles I, executed

3.31 C Charles II

3.32 ✓ 1660

3.33 ✓ The great fire of London   ✓ A plague

3.34 Can you match the famous men with what they did?

Sir Isaac Newton explained how gravity works.
Edmund Halley predicted the return of a comet.
Christopher Wren designed St Paul's Cathedral.
Samuel Pepys wrote a diary.

3.35 C brother
A Catholic

3.36 ✓ because there was no fighting in England

✓ because it guaranteed the power of Parliament

Section 4 A global power

3.37 B The Bill of Rights signed in 1689 said that the king could not raise taxes without the agreement of Parliament

3.38 The American colonies

3.39 ✓ in 1707

3.40 Sir Robert Walpole

3.41 A Bonnie Prince Charlie lost the Battle of Culloden in 1746 and escaped to Europe.

3.42 The Highland Clearances

3.43 At New Year

3.44 C Steam power
A Philosophy
B Economics

3.45 The Bessemer process was used to produce <u>steel</u>.

3.46 True

3.47 ✓ textile

3.48 People who wanted slavery to end are called <u>abolitionists</u>.

3.49 ✓ 1833

3.50 A People living in the American colonies wanted to be independent and have their own government.

3.51 Battle of Trafalgar <u>1805</u>
Battle of Waterloo <u>1815</u>

3.52 C St Andrew
A St George
B St Patrick

3.53 <u>64 years</u>

3.54 400 million

3.55 13 million

3.56 True

3.57 ✓ The Great Western Railway

3.58 A Because of Florence Nightingale and her fellow nurses, fewer wounded soldiers died in hospital during the Crimean War than in earlier wars.

3.59 ✓ A million and a half

3.60 The Reform Act

3.61 The <u>Boers</u>

3.62 *Just So Stories* or *The Jungle Book*

Section 5 The 20th century

3.63 ✓ old age pensions ✓ free school meals

3.64 India

3.65 B In 1922 Ireland became two countries: the Irish Free State had its own government, and Northern Ireland remained part of the UK.

3.66 C First BBC radio broadcasts   1922
B Start of the Great Depression   1929
A First regular television service   1936

3.67 ✓ Dunkirk, France

3.68 The Spitfire and the Hurricane were the most important planes in the Battle of <u>Britain</u>.

Section 6 Britain since 1945

3.69 ✓ Clement Attlee

3.70 India, Pakistan or Sri Lanka

3.71 | Richard A Butler | The Education Act 1944 |
|---|---|
| | Free secondary education in England and Wales |
| William Beveridge | Wrote the report that led to the creation of the welfare state |
| Clement Attlee | Led the government that nationalised the railways, coal mines and gas, electricity and water supplies |
| Nye Bevan | Led the establishment of the National Health Service |

3.72 True

3.73 During the 1950s, centres were set up in the <u>West Indies</u> to recruit people to drive buses.

Textile and engineering firms from the north of England and the Midlands sent agents to India and Pakistan to find workers.

3.74 A New laws in the 1960s made it easier to get an abortion or a divorce in England, Scotland and Wales.

3.75

Inventor	Famous for
Technology and electronics	
John Logie Baird	**Television**
Sir Robert Watson-Watt	Radar
Sir Bernard Lovell	Astronomy, Jodrell Bank
Alan Turing	**Turing machine** (early computer)
Sir Frank Whittle	Jet engine
Sir Peter Mansfield	MRI (magnetic resonance imaging) scanner
Sir Tim Berners-Lee	World Wide Web
Biology and medicine	
John Macleod	Discovering insulin
Francis Crick	**DNA**
Sir Robert Edwards and Patrick Steptoe	In-vitro fertilisation (IVF)
James Goodfellow	**ATM/cash machine**
Sir Ian Wilmut and Keith Campbell	**Cloning Dolly the sheep**

3.76 True

3.77 The UK joined the European Economic Community (EEC) in 1973.

3.78 ✓ Sold the nationalised industries

✓ Fought a war with Argentina

3.79 False

3.80 The Former Republic of Yugoslavia, Iraq or Afghanistan.

3.81 After the General Election in May 2010 the Conservatives and Liberal Democrat parties formed a <u>coalition</u> government.

Answers to revision questions

1 Skara Brae
2 Boudicca
3 William, Duke of Normandy or William the Conqueror
4 Robert the Bruce
5 Clans
6 1215
7 The Canterbury Tales
8 Henry VII
9 Because they opposed the rule of the Protestant government
10 They had not agreed to the execution of Charles I and declared his son, Charles II, to be king
11 The Royal Society
12 The first Prime Minister
13 Robert Burns
14 To work in the mining and manufacturing industries
15 The Bill of Rights
16 The slave trade
17 France
18 The United Kingdom of Great Britain and Ireland
19 George and Robert Stephenson, and Isambard Kingdom Brunel
20 Potato
21 The right to vote for men
22 The Nobel Prize for Literature
23 The First World War
24 Hitler's invasion of Poland
25 Dylan Thomas

26 The Beatles or The Rolling Stones
27 New laws gave women the right to equal pay and it became illegal to discriminate against women
28 In the 1970s
29 Blair or Tony Blair
30 Conservatives and Liberal Democrats

CHAPTER FOUR

A modern, thriving society

In this chapter you will read the official study material about society in the UK today. You will learn more about the nations of the UK, about the many different groups of people who now live here, their traditions, religions and <u>ethnic</u> backgrounds and how they like to enjoy their leisure time.

This chapter is divided into six sections, as follows:

- **Section 1** The UK today
- **Section 2** Religion
- **Section 3** Customs and traditions
- **Section 4** Sport
- **Section 5** Arts and culture
- **Section 6** Leisure

SECTION 1 The UK today

In this section you will read about:

- the nations of the UK
- UK currency
- languages and dialects
- how the population has grown and changed
- the different ethnic groups in the UK
- equal rights for all

The UK today is a more diverse society than it was 100 years ago, in both ethnic and religious terms. Post-war immigration means that nearly 10% of the population has a parent or grandparent born outside the UK. The UK continues to be a <u>multinational</u> and <u>multiracial</u> society with a rich and varied culture. This section will tell you about the different parts of the UK and some of the important places. It will also explain some of the UK's traditions and customs and some of the popular activities that take place.

The nations of the UK

The UK is located in the north west of Europe. The longest distance on the mainland is from John O' Groats on the north coast of Scotland to Land's End in the south-west corner of England. It is about 870 miles (approximately 1,400 kilometres).

Most people live in towns and cities but much of Britain is still countryside. Many people continue to visit the countryside for holidays and for leisure activities such as walking, camping and fishing.

Cities of the UK

Below is a list of 20 of the major cities in the UK and the capital cities of the UK, Scotland, Wales and Northern Ireland.

England
London
Birmingham
Liverpool
Leeds
Sheffield
Bristol
Manchester
Bradford
Newcastle Upon Tyne
Plymouth
Southampton
Norwich

Wales
Cardiff
Swansea
Newport

Northern Ireland
Belfast

Scotland
Edinburgh
Glasgow
Dundee
Aberdeen

Capital cities
The capital city of the UK is London.
Scotland The capital city of Scotland is Edinburgh.
Wales The capital city of Wales is Cardiff.
Northern Ireland The capital city of Northern Ireland is Belfast.

 Check your learning

4.1 Which of the following statements is correct?

A Nearly 40% of the population has a parent or grandparent born outside the UK.

B Nearly 10% of the population has a parent or grandparent born outside the UK.

4.2   Can you match the countries with their capital cities?

☐ England   A Belfast

☐ Northern Ireland   B Cardiff

☐ Scotland   C London

☐ Wales   D Edinburgh

UK currency

The currency in the UK is the pound sterling (symbol £). There are 100 pence in a pound. The denominations (values) of currency are:

     coins: 1p, 2p, 5p, 20p, 50p, £1 and £2
     notes: £5, £10, £20, £50

Northern Ireland and Scotland have their own banknotes, which are valid everywhere in the UK. However, shops and businesses do not have to accept them.

Check your learning

4.3   Which **four** denominations (values) are on UK banknotes? Write them in the boxes below.

£   £   £   £

Languages and dialects

There are many variations in language in the different parts of the UK. The English language has many accents and <u>dialects</u>. In Wales, many people speak Welsh – a completely different language from English – and it is taught in schools and universities. In Scotland, Gaelic (again, a different language) is spoken in some parts of the Highlands and Islands, and in Northern Ireland some people speak Irish Gaelic.

Check your learning

4.4 Write down the name of the non-English language spoken in the following places:

Wales _____

Parts of the Scottish Highlands and Islands _____

Northern Ireland _____

Find out more

All school children in Wales learn to speak the Welsh language. Some go to schools where all the teaching is in Welsh.

⊞ Population

The table below shows how the population of the UK has changed over time.

Population growth in the UK	
Year	**Population**
1600	Just over 4 million
1700	5 million
1801	8 million
1851	20 million
1901	40 million
1951	50 million
1998	57 million
2005	Just under 60 million
2010	Just over 62 million
Source: National Statistics	

Population growth has been faster in more recent years. <u>Migration</u> into the UK and longer life expectancy have played a part in population growth.

The population is very unequally distributed over the four parts of the UK. England more or less consistently makes up 84% of the total population, Wales around 5%, Scotland just over 8%, and Northern Ireland less than 3%.

An ageing population

People in the UK are living longer than ever before. This is due to improved living standards and better health care. There are now a record number of people aged 85 and over. This has an impact on the cost of pensions and health care.

Check your learning

4.5   Is the statement below **True** or **False**?

People in the UK are living longer than in the past because they have improved living conditions and better healthcare.

4.6   Look at the map below and write the percentage of people in each of the four parts of the UK in the boxes.

⊞ Ethnic diversity

The UK population is ethnically diverse and changing rapidly, especially in large cities such as London. It is not always easy to get an exact picture of the ethnic origin of all the population.

There are people in the UK with ethnic origins from all over the world. In surveys, the most common ethnic description chosen is white, which includes people of European, Australian, Canadian, New Zealand and American descent. Other significant groups are those of Asian, black and mixed <u>descent</u>. ⊞

Check your learning

4.7 In surveys, which ethnic description do **most** people choose?

☐ Asian   ☐ Black   ☐ Mixed descent   ☐ White

⊞ An equal society

Within the UK, it is a legal requirement that men and women should not be discriminated against because of their gender or because they are, or are not, married. They have equal rights to work, own property, marry and divorce. If they are married, both parents are equally responsible for their children.

Women in Britain today make up about half the workforce. On average, girls leave school with better qualifications. More women than men study at university.

Employment opportunities for women are much greater than they were in the past. Women work in all sectors of the economy and there are more women in high-level positions than ever before, including senior managers in traditionally male-dominated occupations. Alongside this, men now work in more varied jobs than they did in the past.

It is no longer expected that women should stay at home and not work. Women often continue to work after having children. In many families today, both partners work and both share responsibility for childcare and <u>household chores</u>. ⊞

Check your learning

4.8 Is the following statement **True** or **False**?

Boys leave school with better qualifications than girls and more men than women study at university.

Find out more

© Yuri Arcurs / Shutterstock.com

Although women in Britain make up about half the workforce, there are still not enough women in the highest positions in companies. Only 16% of the top companies in the UK have female directors. Over 40% of the directors in similar companies in Norway are women.

Check your understanding

Now that you have finished Section 1, what can you remember about the following?

- The capital cities of the UK
- Native languages other than English spoken in parts of the UK
- How the population of the UK has grown and changed
- That men and women should be treated as equals by law
- The currency used in the UK

Study tip

Write brief notes about each of the topics or try telling someone else about some of them.

Study tip

To help you remember the names of the cities on the map below, find out something about each one. There are plenty of websites with information about them, you can have a look at books in your local library or ask for information from a tourist office. For example, Aberdeen in Scotland is famous for North Sea oil, Birmingham for canals and Liverpool for the Beatles.

© Creative Jen Designs / Shutterstock.com

SECTION 2 Religion

In this section you will read about the following:

■ **Christianity, the main religion in the UK**

■ **the Anglican Church, also known as the Church of England, and its position as the Church of the state in England (also called the 'established Church')**

■ **the Presbyterian Church, the national Church of Scotland, and other Christian Churches**

■ **some of the other religions in the UK**

■ **saints of England, Scotland, Wales and Northern Ireland**

The UK is historically a Christian country. In the 2009 Citizenship Survey, 70% of people identified themselves as Christian. Much smaller proportions identified themselves as Muslim (4%), Hindu (2%), Sikh (1%), Jewish or Buddhist (both less than 0.5%), and 2% of people followed another religion. There are religious buildings for other religions all over the UK. This includes Islamic mosques, Hindu temples, Jewish synagogues, Sikh gurdwaras and Buddhist temples. However, everyone has the legal right to choose their religion, or to choose not to practise a religion. In the Citizenship Survey, 21% of people said that they had no religion.

Christian churches

In England there is a constitutional link between Church and state. The official Church of the state is the Church of England (called the Anglican Church in other countries and the Episcopal Church in Scotland and the United States). It is a Protestant Church and has existed since the Reformation in the 1530s (see pages 55–56 for an explanation).

The monarch is the head of the Church of England. The spiritual leader of the Church of England is the Archbishop of Canterbury. The monarch has the right to select the Archbishop and other senior church officials, but usually the choice is made by the Prime Minister and a committee appointed by the Church. Several Church of England bishops sit in the House of Lords (see page 228).

In Scotland, the national Church is the Church of Scotland, which is a Presbyterian Church. It is governed by ministers and elders. The chairperson of the General Assembly of the Church of Scotland is the Moderator, who is appointed for one year only and often speaks on behalf of that Church.

There is no established Church in Wales or Northern Ireland.

Other Protestant Christian groups in the UK are Baptists, Methodists, Presbyterians and Quakers. There are also other denominations of Christianity, the biggest of which is Roman Catholic.

Find out more

The Church of Scotland is run democratically. **Ministers**, who are similar to priests, lead Church services and are supported by members of the church called **elders**. Every year ministers and elders are chosen to meet for a week at a General Assembly in Edinburgh where they discuss Church law and other important matters. They elect a **moderator** who chairs, or manages, the General Assembly meeting and represents the Church for a year. Since 1968 all positions in the Church of Scotland have been open to women and there have been a couple of female moderators in recent years.

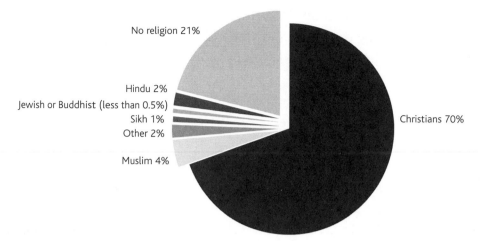

No religion 21%

Hindu 2%
Jewish or Buddhist (less than 0.5%)
Sikh 1%
Other 2%

Christians 70%

Muslim 4%

Fig 4.1 Religions in the UK

 ## Check your learning

4.9 Read the statements below and decide which two are correct.

In the 2009 Citizenship Survey:

A 50% of people said they were Christian
B 21% of people said they had no religion
C 4% of people said they were Muslim
D 2% of people said they were Buddhist

4.10 Complete the following statement using one of the words below

Baptist   Methodist   Presbyterian   Quaker

The Church of Scotland is a _____ Church.

Find out more

The Citizenship Survey is carried out every two years. It asks a sample of UK residents – including people of different ages, genders and ethnic backgrounds – questions on many aspects of their lives. Topics include religion, <u>volunteering</u>, family life, feelings about their local communities and any <u>discrimination</u> they may have experienced.

Study tip

The spider diagram below gives you a summary of the information on the Church of England in the form of a spider diagram. If it helps you remember the information, make your own spider diagrams about the other topics in the study material. Use drawings and colour to make the most important information stand out.

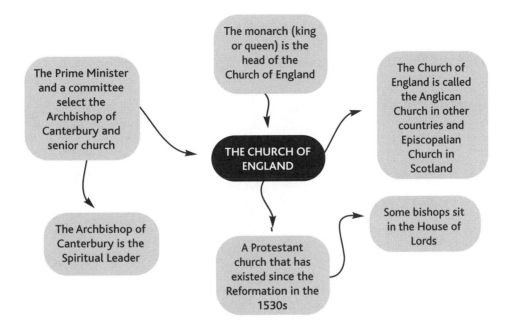

Patron saints' days

England, Scotland, Wales and Northern Ireland each have a national <u>saint</u>, called a patron saint. Each saint has a special day:

- **1 March:**   St David's Day, Wales
- **17 March:**   St Patrick's Day, Northern Ireland
- **23 April:**   St George's Day, England
- **30 November** St Andrew's Day, Scotland

Only Scotland and Northern Ireland have their patron saint's day as an official holiday (although in Scotland not all businesses and offices will close). Events are held across Scotland, Northern Ireland and the rest of the country, especially where there are a lot of people of Scottish, Northern Irish and Irish heritage.

Check your learning

4.11 Is the following statement **True** or **False?**

St George's Day on 23 April is an official holiday in England.

Find out more

Nobody knows the truth about St George, but there is a story that he killed a dragon. Some people believe that the dragon represents both Satan and the Roman Empire.

SECTION 3 Customs and traditions

In this section you will read about the following:

■ the main Christian festivals that are celebrated in the UK

■ other religions and religious festivals that are important in the UK

■ some other events that are celebrated in the UK

■ what a bank holiday is

🇬🇧 The main Christian festivals

Christmas Day, 25 December, celebrates the birth of Jesus Christ. It is a public holiday. Many Christians go to church on Christmas Eve (24 December) or on Christmas Day itself.

Christmas is celebrated in a traditional way. People usually spend the day at home and eat a special meal, which often includes roast turkey, Christmas pudding and mince pies. They give gifts, send cards and decorate their houses. Christmas is a special time for children. Very young children believe that Father Christmas (also known as Santa Claus) brings them presents during the night before Christmas Day. Many people decorate a tree in their home.

© Pack-Shot / Shutterstock.com

Traditional Christmas crib scene

Boxing Day is the day after Christmas Day and is a public holiday.

Easter takes place in March or April. It marks the death of Jesus Christ on Good Friday and his rising from the dead on Easter Sunday. Both Good Friday and the following Monday, called Easter Monday, are public holidays.

The 40 days before Easter are called Lent. It is a time when Christians take time to reflect and prepare for Easter. Traditionally, people would fast during this period and today many people will give something up, like a favourite food. The day before Lent starts is called Shrove Tuesday, or Pancake Day. People eat pancakes, which were traditionally made to use up foods such as eggs, fat and milk before fasting. Lent begins on Ash Wednesday. There are church services where Christians are marked with an ash cross on their forehead as a symbol of death and sorrow for sin.

© Kati Molin / Shutterstock.com

Easter eggs

Easter is also celebrated by people who are not religious. 'Easter eggs' are chocolate eggs often given as presents at Easter as a symbol of new life.

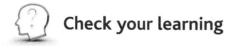

Check your learning

4.12 Can you match the festival with the event it celebrates?

The birth of Jesus Christ	A Easter
The death of Jesus Christ	B Christmas
Jesus Christ rising from the dead	C Good Friday

🇬🇧 Other religious festivals

Diwali lights

Diwali normally falls in October or November and lasts for five days. It is often called the Festival of Lights. It is celebrated by Hindus and Sikhs. It celebrates the victory of good over evil and the gaining of knowledge. There are different stories about how the festival came about. There is a famous celebration of Diwali in Leicester.

Menorah

Hannukah is in November or December and is celebrated for eight days. It is to remember the Jews' struggle for religious freedom. On each day of the festival a candle is lit on a stand of eight candles (called a menorah) to remember the story of the festival, where oil should have lasted only a day but did so for eight.

Eid al-Fitr celebrates the end of Ramadan, when Muslims have fasted for a month. They thank Allah for giving them the strength to complete the fast. The date when it takes place changes every year. Muslims attend special services and meals.

Eid ul Adha remembers that the prophet Ibrahim was willing to sacrifice his son when God ordered him to. It reminds Muslims of their own commitment to God. Many Muslims sacrifice an animal to eat during this festival. In Britain this has to be done in a <u>slaughterhouse</u>.

Vaishakhi (also spelled Baishakhi) is a Sikh festival which celebrates the founding of the Sikh community known as the Khalsa. It is celebrated on 14 April each year with parades, dancing and singing. 🇬🇧

? Check your learning

4.13 Can you match the following festivals and the religions to which they belong?

| Hindu | Jewish | Muslim | Sikh |

| A Eid al-Fitr | B Vaisakhi | C Diwali | D Hannukah |

🇬🇧 Other festivals and traditions

New Year, 1 January, is a public holiday. People usually celebrate on the night of 31 December (called New Year's Eve). In Scotland, 31 December is called Hogmanay and 2 January is also a public holiday. For some Scottish people, Hogmanay is a bigger holiday than Christmas.

Valentine's Day, 14 February, is when lovers exchange cards and gifts. Sometimes people send anonymous cards to someone the secretly admire.

April Fool's Day, 1 April, is a day when people play jokes on each other until midday. The television and newspapers often have stories that are April Fool jokes.

Mothering Sunday (or Mother's Day) is the Sunday three weeks before Easter. Children send cards or buy gifts for their mothers.

Father's Day is the third Sunday in June. Children send cards or buy gifts for their fathers.

Halloween, 31 October, is an ancient festival and has roots in the <u>Pagan</u> festival to mark the beginning of winter. Young people will often dress up in frightening costumes to play 'trick or treat'. People give them treats to stop them playing tricks on them. A lot of people carve lanterns out of pumpkins and put a candle inside.

Bonfire Night, 5 November, is an occasion when people in Great Britain set off fireworks at home or in special displays. The origin of this celebration was an event in 1605, when a group of Catholics led by Guy Fawkes failed in their plan to kill the Protestant king with a bomb in the Houses of Parliament.

Remembrance Day, 11 November, commemorates those who died fighting for the UK and its allies. Originally it commemorated the dead of the First World War, which ended on 11 November, 1918. People wear poppies (the red flower found on the battlefields of the First World War). At 11.00 am there is a two-minute silence and <u>wreaths</u> are laid at the <u>Cenotaph</u> in Whitehall, London.

Bank holidays

As well as those mentioned previously, there are other public holidays each year called bank holidays, when banks and many other businesses are closed for the day. These are of no religious significance. They are at the beginning of May, in late May or early June, and in August. In Northern Ireland, the <u>anniversary</u> of the Battle of the Boyne in July is also a public holiday. 🇬🇧

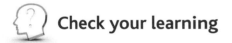 **Check your learning**

4.14 What is the name of the festival when lovers exchange cards and gifts on 14 February?

- ☐ St Valentine's Day
- ☐ Bonfire Night
- ☐ Halloween
- ☐ Remembrance Day

4.15 Is the following statement **True** or **False**?

Banks are the only businesses that close on a bank holiday.

Find out more

On 1 April 1957, the BBC produced a television documentary that convinced people there were spaghetti crops growing in Switzerland.

Study tip

To help you remember the dates in this section, you could make a timeline from 1 January to 31 December. Why not link these dates to dates that are important to you such as your birthday, a wedding anniversary, or the date that you arrived in the UK.

You might find it helpful to imagine a picture of an event and include the date in the picture; for example, a heart with 14 February in it to help you remember the date for St Valentine's Day. Another example could be a bonfire with 5 November or a firework to remember Bonfire Night.

Be aware that the dates of the Muslim festivals change every year. The dates of Hannukah and Diwali also change but only by a few days.

We have started it for you:

Festival	Date	Your dates
New Year	January 1	
St Valentine's Day	February 14	

Check your understanding

Now that you have read Section 3, what can you remember about the following?

- The main Christian festivals that are celebrated in the UK and when they happen
- Other religious festivals that are important in the UK
- Other events and festivals that are celebrated in the UK
- The festivals that are celebrated in some parts of the UK but not others
- What a bank holiday is

SECTION 4 Sport

In this section you will read about the following:

- **sports that are popular in the UK**
- **some famous sportsmen and women from the UK.**

Sports of all kinds play an important part in many people's lives. There are several sports that are particularly popular in the UK. Many sporting events take place at major stadiums such as Wembley Stadium in London and the Millennium Stadium in Cardiff.

Local governments and private companies provide sports facilities such as swimming pools, tennis courts, football pitches, dry ski slopes and gymnasiums. Many famous sports, including cricket, football, lawn tennis, golf and rugby, began in Britain.

The UK has hosted the Olympic Games on three occasions: 1908, 1948 and 2012. The main Olympic site for the 2012 Games was in Stratford, East London. The British team was very successful, across a wide range of Olympic sports, finishing third in the medal table.

The Paralympic Games for 2012 were also hosted in London. The Paralympics have their origin in the work of Dr Sir Ludwig Guttman, a German refugee, at the Stoke Mandeville hospital in Buckinghamshire. Dr Guttman developed new methods of treatment for people with spinal injuries and encouraged patients to take part in exercise and sport.

© pcruciatti / Shutterstock.com

Women's hurdles race

Check your learning

4.16 In which of the following capital cities will you find the Millennium Stadium where many sporting events take place?

☐ A Belfast ☐ B Cardiff

☐ C Edinburgh ☐ D London

4.17 Is the following statement **True** or **False**?

The UK hosted the Olympic Games for the third time in 1948.

⊞ Notable British sportsmen and women

Sir Roger Bannister (1929–) was the first man in the world to run a mile in under four minutes, in 1954.

Sir Jackie Stewart (1939–) is a Scottish former racing driver who won the Formula 1 world championship three times.

Bobby Moore (1941–93) captained the English football team that won the World Cup in 1966.

Sir Ian Botham (1955–) captained the English cricket team and holds a number of English Test cricket records, both for batting and for bowling.

Jayne Torville (1957–) and **Christopher Dean** (1958-) won gold medals for ice dancing at the Olympic Games in 1984 and in four consecutive world championships.

Sir Steve Redgrave (1962–) won gold medals in rowing in five consecutive Olympic Games and is one of Britain's greatest Olympians.

Baroness Tanni Grey-Thompson (1969–) is an athlete who uses a wheelchair and won 16 Paralympic medals, including 11 gold medals, in races over five Paralympic Games. She won the London Marathon six times and broke a total of 30 world records.

Dame Kelly Holmes (1970–) won two gold medals for running in the 2004 Olympic Games. She has held a number of British and European records.

Dame Ellen MacArthur (1976–) is a yachtswoman and in 2004 became the fastest person to sail around the world singlehanded.

Sir Chris Hoy (1976–) is a Scottish cyclist who has won six gold and one silver Olympic medals. He has also won 11 world championship titles.

David Weir (1979–) is a Paralympian who uses a wheelchair and has won six gold medals over two Paralympic Games. He has also won the London Marathon six times.

Bradley Wiggins (1980–) is a cyclist. In 2012 he became the first Briton to win the Tour de France. He has won several Olympic medals, including gold medals in the 2004, 2008 and 2012 Olympic Games.

Mo Farah (1983–) is a British distance runner, born in Somalia. He won gold medals in the 2012 Olympics for the 5,000 and 10,000 metres and is the first Briton to win the Olympic gold medal in the 10,000 metres.

Jessica Ennis (1986–) is an athlete. She won the 2012 Olympic gold medal in the heptathlon, which includes seven different track and field events. She also holds a number of British athletics records.

Andy Murray (1987–) is a Scottish tennis player who in 2012 won the men's singles in the US Open. He is the first British man to win a singles title in a Grand Slam tournament since 1936. In the same year, he won Olympic gold and silver medals and was runner-up in the men's singles at Wimbledon (see page 180).

Ellie Simmonds (1994–) is a Paralympian who won gold medals for swimming at the 2008 and 2012 Paralympic Games and holds a number of world records. She was the youngest member of the British team at the 2008 Games.

 **Check your learning**

4.18 Can you match the following sports men and women with their sport?

Bradley Wiggins	Running
Ellie Simmonds	Cycling
Mo Farah	Rowing
Sir Steve Redgrave	Swimming

Cricket

Cricket <u>originated</u> in England and is now played in many countries. Games can last up to five days but still result in a draw! The <u>idiosyncratic</u> nature of the game and its complex laws are said to reflect the best of British <u>character</u> and sense of <u>fair play</u>. You may come across <u>expressions</u> such as 'rain stopped play', 'batting on a sticky wicket', 'playing a straight bat', 'bowled a googly' or 'it's just not cricket' which have passed into everyday usage. The most famous competition is the Ashes, which is a series of Test matches played between England and Australia.

© Najiyyer / Shutterstock.com

Football

Football is the UK's most popular sport. It has a long history in the UK and the first professional football clubs were formed in the late 19th century.

David Beckham

© beltsazar / Shutterstock.com

England, Scotland, Wales and Northern Ireland each have separate leagues in which clubs representing different towns and cities compete. The English Premier League attracts a huge international audience. Many of the best players in the world play in the Premier League. Many UK teams also compete in competitions such as the UEFA (Union of European Football Associations) Champions League. Most towns and cities have a professional club and people take great pride in supporting their home team. There can be great rivalry between different football clubs and among fans.

Each country in the UK has its own national team that competes with other national teams across the world in tournaments such as the FIFA (Fédération Internationale de Football Association) World Cup and the UEFA European Football Championships. England's only international tournament victory was the World Cup of 1966, hosted in the UK.

Football is also a popular sport to play in many local communities, with people playing amateur games every week in parks all over the UK.

Rugby

Rugby originated in England in the early 19th century and is very popular in the UK today. There are two different types of rugby, which have different rules: union and league. Both have separate leagues and national teams in England, Wales, Scotland and Northern Ireland (who play with the Irish Republic). Teams from all countries compete on a range of competitions. The most famous rugby union competition is the Six Nations Championship between England, Ireland, Scotland, Wales, France and Italy. The Super League is the most well-known rugby league (club) competition.

© Neil Balderson / Shutterstock.com

Horse racing

There is a very long history of horse racing in Britain, with evidence of events taking place as far back as Roman times. The sport has a long association with royalty. There are racecourses all over the UK. Famous horse-racing events include: Royal Ascot, a five-day race meeting in Berkshire attended by members of the Royal Family; the Grand National at Aintree near Liverpool; and the Scottish Grand National at Ayr. There is a National Horseracing Museum in Newmarket, Suffolk.

Golf

The modern game of golf can be traced back to 15th century Scotland. It is a popular sport played socially as well as professionally. There are public and private golf courses all over the UK. St Andrews in Scotland is known as the home of golf. The Open Championship is the only 'Major' tournament held outside the United States. It is hosted by a different golf course every year.

Tennis

Modern tennis evolved in England in the late 19th century. The first tennis club was founded in Leamington Spa in 1872. The most famous tournament hosted in Britain is The Wimbledon Championships, which takes place each year at the All England Lawn Tennis and Croquet Club. It is the oldest tennis tournament in the world and the only 'Grand Slam' event played on grass.

Andy Murray

Water sports

Sailing continues to be popular in the UK, reflecting our maritime <u>heritage</u>. A British sailor, Sir Francis Chichester, was the first person to sail single-handed around the world, in 1966/67. Two years later, Sir Robin-Knox Johnston became the first person to do this without stopping. Many sailing events are held throughout the UK, the most famous of which is at Cowes on the Isle of Wight.

Rowing is also popular, both as a leisure activity and as a competitive sport. There is a popular yearly race on the Thames between Oxford and Cambridge Universities.

Skiing

Skiing is increasingly popular in the UK. Many people go abroad to ski and there are also dry ski slopes throughout the UK. Skiing on snow may also be possible during the winter. There are five ski centres in Scotland, as well as Europe's longest dry ski slope near Edinburgh.

Motor sports

There is a long history of motor sport in the UK, for both cars and motor cycles. Motor-car racing in the UK started in 1902. The UK continues to be a world leader in the development and manufacture of motor-sport technology. A Formula 1 Grand Prix event is held in the UK and a number of British Grand Prix drivers have won the Formula 1 Grand Prix World Championship. Recent British winners include Damon Hill, Lewis Hamilton and Jenson Button.

© Natursports / Shutterstock.com

Lewis Hamilton

 **Check your learning**

4.19 Tick the boxes beside the three sports in the list below that began in Britain:

☐ Cricket   ☐ Horse racing   ☐ Golf
☐ Lawn tennis   ☐ Motor sports   ☐ Skiing
☐ Water sports

SECTION 5 Arts and culture

In this section you will read about the following:

■ **music and some British composers and musicians**

■ **theatre, including musicals and pantomimes**

■ **art, famous British artists and galleries**

■ **architecture**

■ **fashion and design**

■ **literature, famous British writers and poets**

🇬🇧 Music

Music is an important part of British culture, with a rich and varied <u>heritage</u>. It ranges from classical music to modern pop. There are many different venues and musical events that take place across the UK.

The Proms is an eight-week summer season of <u>orchestral classical</u> music that takes place in various venues, including the Royal Albert Hall in London. It has been organised by the British Broadcasting Corporation (BBC) since 1927. The Last Night of the Proms is the most well-known concert and (along with others in the series) is broadcast on television.

Classical music has been popular in the UK for many centuries. **Henry Purcell (1659–95)** was the <u>organist</u> at Westminster Abbey. He wrote church music, operas and other pieces, and developed a British style distinct from that elsewhere in Europe. He continues to be influential on British composers.

The German-born <u>composer</u> **George Fredrick Handel (1695–1759)** spent many years in the UK and became a British citizen in 1727. He wrote the *Water Music* for King George I and *Music for the Royal Fireworks* for his son, George II. Both these pieces continue to be very popular. Handel also wrote an <u>oratorio</u>, *Messiah*, which is sung regularly by choirs, often at Easter time.

More recently, important composers include **Gustav Holst (1874–1934),** whose work includes *The Planets*, a suite of pieces themed around the planets of the solar system. He adapted *Jupiter*, part of the *Planets* suite, as the tune for *I vow to thee my country*, a popular <u>hymn</u> in British churches.

Sir Edward Elgar (1857–1934) was born in Worcester, England. His best-known work is probably the *Pomp and Circumstances Marches. March No 1 (Land of Hope and Glory)* is usually played at the Last Night of the Proms at the Royal Albert Hall.

Ralph Vaughn Williams (1872–1958) wrote music for orchestras and <u>choirs</u>. He was strongly influenced by traditional English folk music.

Sir William Walton (1902–83) wrote a wide range of music, from film scores to opera. He wrote marches for the coronations of King George VI and Queen Elizabeth II but his best known works are probably *Façade*, which became a ballet, and *Balthazar's Feast*, which is intended to be sung by a large choir.

Benjamin Britten (1913–76) is best known for his operas, which include *Peter Grimes* and *Billy Budd*. He also wrote *A Young Person's Guide to the Orchestra*, which is based on a piece of music by Purcell and introduces the listener to the various different sections of an orchestra. He founded the Aldeburgh festival in Suffolk, which continues to be a popular music event of international importance.

Other types of popular music, including folk music, jazz, pop and rock music, have flourished in Britain since the 20th century. Britain has had an impact on popular music around the world, due to the wide use of the English language, the UK's cultural links with many countries, and British capacity for invention and innovation.

Since the 1960s, British pop music has made one of the most important cultural contributions to life in the UK. Bands including The Beatles and The Rolling Stones continue to have an influence on music both here and abroad. British pop music has continued to <u>innovate</u> – for example, the Punk movement of the late 1970s, and the trend towards boy and girl bands in the 1990s.

There are many large venues that host music events throughout the year, such as: Wembley Stadium; The O2 in Greenwich, south-east London; and the Scottish Exhibition and Conference Centre (SECC) in Glasgow.

Festival season takes place across the UK every summer, with major events in various locations. Famous festivals include Glastonbury, the Isle of Wight Festival and the V Festival. Many bands and solo artists, both well-known and up-and-coming, perform at these events.

The National Eisteddfod of Wales is an annual cultural festival which includes music, dance, art and original performances largely in Welsh. It includes a number of important competitions for Welsh poetry.

The Mercury Music Prize is awarded each September for the best album from the UK and Ireland. The Brit Awards is an annual event that gives awards in a range of categories, such as best British group and best British solo artist.

Check your learning

4.20 Can you match the composers with the pieces of music they wrote?

A George Frederic Handel   ☐ The Planets

B Gustav Holst   ☐ Land of Hope and Glory

C Edward Elgar   ☐ A Young Person's Guide to the Orchestra

D Benjamin Britten   ☐ Water Music

4.21 Without looking at the text, can you remember the name of one of the most famous 1960s bands whose music is still popular today?

Study tip

Many people find that music helps them learn. You may enjoy listening to the music by UK composers and musicians. For classical music you could try BBC Radio 3 or Classic FM. Radio 1 and local radio stations are better for the latest bands. In addition, you can borrow CDs from your local library. Hearing the pieces of music mentioned in the text should help you to remember them and their composers.

🇬🇧 Theatre

There are theatres in most towns and cities throughout the UK, ranging from the large to the small. They are an important part of local communities and often show both professional and amateur productions. London's West End, also know as 'Theatreland', is particularly well known. *The Mousetrap*, a murder-mystery play by Dame Agatha Christie, has been running in the West End since 1952 and has had the longest initial run of any show in history.

There is also a strong tradition of musical theatre in the UK. In the 19th century, Gilbert and Sullivan wrote comic operas, often making fun of popular culture and politics. These operas include *HMS Pinafore, The Pirates of Penzance* and *The Mikado*. Gilbert and Sullivan's work is still often staged by professional and amateur groups. More recently, Andrew Lloyd Webber has written the music for shows which have been popular throughout the world, including, in collaboration with Tim Rice, *Jesus Christ Superstar* and *Evita*, and also *Cats* and *The Phantom of the Opera*.

One British tradition is the pantomime. Many theatres produce a pantomime at Christmas time. They are based on fairy stories and are light-hearted plays with music and comedy, enjoyed by family audiences. One of the traditional characters is the Dame, a woman played by a man. There is often also a pantomime horse or cow played by two actors in the same costume.

The Edinburgh Festival takes place in Edinburgh, Scotland, every summer. It is a series of different arts and cultural festivals, with the biggest and most well-known being the Edinburgh Festival Fringe ('the Fringe'). The Fringe is a showcase of mainly theatre and comedy performances. It often shows experimental work.

The Laurence Olivier Awards take place annually at different venues in London. There are a variety of categories, including best director, best actor and best actress. The awards are named after the British actor Sir Laurence Olivier, later Lord Olivier, who was best known for his roles in various Shakespeare plays. 🏴󠁧󠁢󠁥󠁮󠁧󠁿

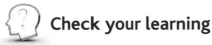 Check your learning

4.22 Which of the following shows has been running in a London West End theatre since 1952?

☐ Cats ☐ Evita ☐ The Mikado ☐ The Mousetrap

4.23 Complete the following sentence:

Every summer a number of arts and cultural festivals are held in Edinburgh, with the biggest being the Edinburgh _____ Festival.

> **Find out more**
>
> Many actors believe it is bad luck to say the name of William Shakespeare's play *Macbeth* and call it *The Scottish Play* (*Macbeth* is set in Scotland).

🏴󠁧󠁢󠁥󠁮󠁧󠁿 Art

During the Middle Ages, most art had a religious theme, particularly wall paintings in churches and <u>illustrations</u> in religious books. Much of this was lost after the Protestant Reformation but wealthy families began to collect other paintings and sculptures. Many of the painters working in Britain in the 16th and 17th centuries were from abroad – for example, Hans Holbein and Sir Anthony Van Dyck. British artists, particularly those painting portraits and landscapes became well known from the 18th century onwards.

Works by British and international artists are displayed in galleries across the UK. Some of the most well-known galleries are The National Gallery, Tate Britain and Tate Modern in London, the National Museum in Cardiff and the National Gallery of Scotland in Edinburgh.

Notable British artists

- **Thomas Gainsborough (1727–88)** was a portrait painter who often painted people in country or garden scenery.

- **David Allan (1744–96)** was a Scottish painter who was best known for painting portraits. One of his most famous works is called *The Origin of Painting*.

- **Joseph Turner (1775–1851)** was an influential landscape painter in a modern style. He is considered the artist who raised the profile of landscape painting.

- **John Constable (1776–1837)** was a landscape painter most famous for his works of Dedham Vale on the Suffolk–Essex border in the east of England.

- **The Pre-Raphaelites** were an important group of artists in the second half of the 19th century. They painted detailed pictures on religious or literary themes in bright colours. The group included Holman Hunt, Dante Gabriel Rossetti and Sir John Millais.

- **Sir John Lavery (1856–1941)** was a very successful Northern Irish portrait painter. His work included painting the Royal Family.

- **Henry Moore (1898–1986)** was an English sculptor and artist. He is best known for his large bronze abstract sculptures.

- **John Petts (1914–91)** was a Welsh artist, best know for his engravings and stained glass.

- **Lucian Freud (1922–2011)** was a German-born British artist. He is best known for his portraits.

■ **David Hockney (1937–)** was an important contributor to the 'pop art' movement of the 1960s and continues to be influential today

The Turner Prize was established in 1984 and celebrates contemporary art. It is named after Joseph Turner. Four works are shortlisted every year and shown at Tate Britain before the winner is announced. The Turner Prize is recognised as one of the most <u>prestigious</u> visual art awards in Europe. Previous winners include Damien Hirst and Richard Wright.

Damien Hirst

Check your learning

4.24 Which two of the following are best known for painting portraits of people?

☐ David Allan   ☐ Joseph Turner
☐ Henry Moore   ☐ Thomas Gainsborough

⚑ Architecture

The architectural heritage of the UK is rich and varied. In the Middle Ages, great cathedrals and churches were built, many of which still stand today. Examples are the cathedrals in Durham, Lincoln, Canterbury and Salisbury. The White Tower is an example of a Norman castle keep, built on the orders of William the Conqueror (see page 40).

Gradually, as the countryside became more peaceful and landowners became richer, the houses of the wealthy became more elaborate and great country houses such as Hardwick Hall in Derbyshire were built.

In the 17th century, Inigo Jones took inspiration from classical architecture to design the Queen's House at Greenwich and the Banqueting Hall in Whitehall in London. Later in the century, Sir Christopher Wren helped develop a British version of the <u>ornate</u> styles popular in Europe in buildings such as the new St Paul's Cathedral.

In the 18th century, simpler designs became popular. The Scottish architect Robert Adam influenced the development of architecture in the UK, Europe and America. He designed the inside decoration as well as the building itself in great houses such as Dumfries House in Scotland. His ideas influenced architects in cities such as Bath where the Royal Crescent was built.

In the 19th century, the medieval 'gothic' style became popular again. As cities expanded, many great public buildings were built in this style. The Houses of Parliament and St Pancras Station were built at this time, as were the town halls in cities such as Manchester and Sheffield.

In the 20th century, Sir Edwin Lutyens had an influence throughout the British Empire. He designed New Delhi to be the seat of government in India. After the First World War, he was responsible for many war memorials throughout the world, including the Cenotaph in Whitehall. The Cenotaph is the site of the annual Remembrance Day service attended by the Queen, politicians and foreign ambassadors (see page 171).

Modern British architects including **Sir Norman Foster**, **Lord** (Richard) **Rogers** and **Dame Zaha Hadid** continue to work on major projects throughout the world as well as within the UK.

Alongside the development of architecture, garden design and landscaping have played an important role in the UK. In the 18th century, **Lancelot 'Capability' Brown** designed the grounds around country houses so that the landscape appeared to be natural, with grass, trees and lakes. He often said that a place had 'capabilities'. Later **Gertrude Jekyll** often worked with **Edwin Lutyens** to design colourful gardens around the houses he designed. Gardens continue to be an important part of homes in the UK. The annual Chelsea Flower Show showcases garden design from Britain and around the world. 🇬🇧

Dame Zaha Hadid's Aquatic Centre for the London 2012 Olympics

© David Burrows / Shutterstock.com

Check your learning

4.25 Can you match the famous building with the architect who designed it?

A Inigo Jones   ☐ The Cenotaph in London
B Christopher Wren   ☐ Dumfries House in Scotland
C Robert Adam   ☐ The Queen's House at Greenwich
D Edwin Lutyens   ☐ St Paul's Cathedral in London

4.26 Who worked with Edwin Lutyens to design colourful gardens around the houses he designed?

☐ Zaha Hadid   ☐ Norman Foster
☐ Gertrude Jekyll   ☐ Richard Rogers

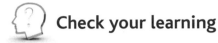 Fashion and design

Britain has produced many great designers, from **Thomas Chippendale** (who designed furniture in the 18th century) to **Clarice Cliff** (who designed Art Deco ceramics), to **Sir Terence Conran** (a 20th-century interior designer). Leading fashion designers of recent years include **Mary Quant, Alexander McQueen** and **Vivienne Westwood.**

Check your learning

4.27 Which of the following statements is correct?

A Alexander McQueen and Vivienne Westwood are leading furniture designers.

B Alexander McQueen and Vivienne Westwood are leading fashion designers.

Literature

The UK has a prestigious literary history and tradition. Several British writers, including the novelist **Sir William Golding**, the poet **Seamus Heaney**, and the playwright **Harold Pinter**, have won the Nobel Prize in Literature. Other authors have become well known in popular fiction. **Agatha Christie**'s detective stories are read all over the world and Ian Fleming's books introduced James Bond. In 2003 *The Lord of the Rings* by **JRR Tolkien** was voted the country's best-loved novel.

The Man Booker Prize for Fiction is awarded annually for the best fiction novel written by an author from the Commonwealth, Ireland or Zimbabwe. It has been awarded since 1968. Past winners include Ian McEwan, Hilary Mantel and Julian Barnes.

Notable authors and writers

Jane Austen (1775–1817) was an English novelist. Her books include *Pride and Prejudice* and *Sense and Sensibility*. Her novels are concerned with marriage and family relationships. Many have been made into television programmes and films.

© Nicku / Shutterstock.com

Charles Dickens (1812–70) wrote a number of very famous novels, including *Oliver Twist* and *Great Expectations*. You will hear <u>references</u> in everyday talk to some of the characters, such as Scrooge (a mean person) or Mr Micawber (always hopeful).

Robert Louis Stevenson (1850–94) wrote books which are still read by adults and children today. His most famous books include *Treasure Island, Kidnapped* and *Dr Jekyll and Mr Hyde*.

Thomas Hardy (1840–1928) was an author and poet. His best-known novels focus on rural society and include *Far from the Madding Crowd* and *Jude the Obscure*.

Sir Arthur Conan Doyle (1859–1930) was a Scottish doctor and writer. He was best known for his stories about Sherlock Holmes, who was one of the first fictional detectives.

Evelyn Waugh (1903–66) wrote satirical novels, including *Decline and Fall* and *Scoop*. He is perhaps best known for *Brideshead Revisited*.

Sir Kingsley Amis (1922–95) was an English novelist and poet. He wrote more than 20 novels. The most well known is *Lucky Jim*.

Graham Greene (1904–91) wrote novels often influenced by his religious beliefs, including *The Heart of the Matter, The Honorary Consul, Brighton Rock* and *Our Man in Havana*.

J K Rowling (1965–) wrote the Harry Potter series of children's books, which have enjoyed huge international success. She now writes fiction for adults as well.

 **Check your learning**

4.28 Can you match the following authors with the books they wrote?

A Jane Austen   ☐ Harry Potter books

B Robert Louis Stevenson   ☐ Sherlock Holmes stories

C Sir Arthur Conan Doyle   ☐ *Pride and Prejudice*

D JK Rowling   ☐ *Treasure Island, Dr Jekyll and Mr Hyde*

⊞ British poets

British poetry is among the richest in the world. The Anglo-Saxon *Beowulf* tells of its hero's battles against monsters and is still translated into modern English. Poems which survive from the Middle Ages include Chaucer's *Canterbury Tales* and a poem called *Sir Gawain and the Green Knight*, about one of the knights at the court of King Arthur.

As well as plays, Shakespeare wrote many sonnets (poems which must be 14 lines long) and some longer poems. As Protestant ideas spread, a number of poets wrote poems inspired by their religious views. One of these was John Milton, who wrote *Paradise Lost*.

Other poets, including William Wordsworth, were inspired by nature. Sir Walter Scott wrote poems inspired by Scotland and the traditional stories and songs from the area on the borders of Scotland and England. He also wrote novels, many of which were set in Scotland.

Poetry was very popular in the 19th century with poets such as William Blake, John Keats, Lord Byron, Percy Shelley, Alfred Lord Tennyson, and Robert and Elizabeth Browning. Later many poets – for example, Wilfred Owen and Siegfried Sassoon – were inspired to write about their experiences in the First World War. More recently, popular poets have included Sir Walter de la Mare, John Masefield, Sir John Betjeman and Ted Hughes.

Some of the best-known poets are buried or commemorated in Poet's Corner in Westminster Abbey.

Some famous lines include:

'O, to be in England now that April's there,
And whoever wakes in England sees, some morning, unaware,
That the lowest boughs and the brushwood sheaf
Round the elm-tree bole are in tiny leaf,
While the chaffinch sings on the orchard bough
In England – Now!'
(Robert Browning, 1812–89 – *Home Thoughts from Abroad*)

'She walks in beauty, like the night
Of cloudless climes and starry skies,
And all that's best of dark and bright
Meet in her aspect and her eyes'
(Lord Byron, 1788–1824 – *She Walks in Beauty*)

'I wander'd lonely as a cloud
That floats on high o'er vales and hills
When all at once I saw a crowd,
A host, of golden daffodils'
(William Wordsworth, 1770–1850 – *The Daffodils*)

'Tyger! Tyger! burning bright
In the forests of the night,
What immortal hand or eye
Could frame thy fearful symmetry?'
(William Blake, 1757–1827 – *The Tyger*)

'What passing-bells for these who die as cattle?
Only the monstrous anger of the guns.
Only the stuttering rifles' rapid rattle
Can patter out their hasty orisons.'
(Wilfred Owen, 1893–1918 – *Anthem For Doomed Youth*)

Check your learning

4.29 Without looking at the text, can you name **one** of the poets who wrote about his experiences during the war?

Check your understanding

Now you have read Section 5, what can you remember about the following?

■ Music in the UK and some British composers and bands

■ Theatre, including musicals and pantomimes

■ Important arts and culture events that take place in the UK

■ Art, famous British artists and galleries

■ Architecture

■ Fashion and design

■ Literature, famous British writers and poets

■ Prizes and awards in arts and culture

SECTION 6 Leisure

In this section you will find out more about leisure activities in the UK. You will read about the following:

■ **gardening, shopping, cooking and traditional foods**

■ **the development of the British film industry**

■ **British comedy, television and radio**

■ **some of the places of interest to visit in the UK**

People in the UK spend their leisure time in many different ways.

🇬🇧 Gardening

A lot of people have gardens at home and will spend their free time looking after them. Some people rent additional land called 'an <u>allotment</u>', where they grow fruit and vegetables. Gardening and flower shows range from major national exhibitions to small local events. Many towns have garden centres selling plants and gardening equipment. There are famous gardens to visit throughout the UK, including Kew Gardens, Hidcote and Sissinghurst in England, Crathes Castle and Inverary Castle in Scotland, Bodnant Garden in Wales, and Mount Stewart in Northern Ireland.

The countries that make up the UK all have flowers which are particularly <u>associated</u> with them and which are sometimes worn on national saints' days:

 England – the rose

 Scotland – the thistle

Wales – the daffodil

 Northern Ireland – the shamrock

Shopping

© Baloncici / Shutterstock.com

There are many different places to go shopping in the UK. Most towns and cities have a central shopping area, which is called the town centre. Undercover shopping centres are also common – these might be in town centres or on the outskirts of a town or city. Most shops in the UK are open seven days a week, although trading hours on Sundays and public holidays are generally reduced. Many towns also have markets on one or more days a week, where stall holders sell a variety of goods.

Cooking and food

Many people in the UK enjoy cooking. They often invite each other to their homes for dinner. A wide variety of food is eaten in the UK because of the country's rich cultural heritage and <u>diverse population</u>.

Traditional foods

There are a variety of foods that are traditionally associated with different parts of the UK:

- **England:** Roast beef, which is served with potatoes, vegetables, Yorkshire puddings (batter that is baked in the oven) and other accompaniments. Fish and chips are also popular.

- **Wales:** Welsh cakes – a traditional Welsh snack made from flour, dried fruits and spices, and served either hot or cold.

- **Scotland:** Haggis – a sheep's stomach stuffed with offal, suet, onions and oatmeal.

- **Northern Ireland:** Ulster fry – a fried meal with bacon, eggs, sausage, black pudding, white pudding, tomatoes, mushrooms, soda bread and potato bread.

Check your learning

4.30 Complete the table below. We have started it for you:

Country	Wales		Northern Ireland	
National flower or plant			Shamrock	Thistle
Traditional food		Roast beef and Yorkshire pudding		

British film industry

The UK has had a major influence on modern cinema.

Films were first shown publicly in the UK in 1896 and film screenings very quickly became popular. From the beginning, British film makers became famous for clever special effects and this continues to be an area of British expertise. From the early days of the cinema, British actors have worked in both the UK and USA. Sir Charles (Charlie) Chaplin became famous in silent movies for his tramp character and was one of many British actors to make a career in Hollywood.

British studios flourished in the 1930s. Eminent directors included Sir Alexander Korda and Sir Alfred Hitchcock, who later left for Hollywood and remained an important film director until his death in 1980. During the Second World War, British movies (for example, *In Which We Serve*) played an important part in boosting morale. Later, British directors including Sir David

Lean and Ridley Scott found great success both in the UK and internationally.

The 1950s and 1960s were a high point for British comedies, including *Passport to Pimlico*, *The Ladykillers* and, later, the *Carry On* films.

Many of the films now produced in the UK are made by foreign companies, using British expertise. Some of the most <u>commercially successful</u> films of all time, including the two <u>highest-grossing</u> <u>film franchises</u> (Harry Potter and James Bond), have been produced in the UK. Ealing Studios has a claim to being the oldest continuously working film studio facility in the world. Britain continues to be particularly strong in special effects and <u>animation</u>. One example is the work of Nick Park, who has won four Oscars for his animated films, including three for films <u>featuring</u> Wallace and Gromit.

Actors such as Sir Laurence Olivier, David Niven, Sir Rex Harrison and Richard Burton starred in a wide variety of popular films. British actors continue to be popular and to win awards throughout the world. Recent British actors to have won Oscars include Colin Firth, Sir Anthony Hopkins, Dame Judi Dench, Kate Winslet and Tilda Swinton.

The annual British Academy Film Awards, hosted by the British Academy of Film and Television Arts (BAFTA), are the British equivalent of Oscars.

© Featureflash / Shutterstock.com

Dame Judi Dench

Some famous British films

- *The 39 Steps* (1935), directed by Alfred Hitchcock
- *Brief Encounter* (1945), directed by David Lean
- *The Third Man* (1949), directed by Carol Reed
- *The Belles of St Trinian's* (1954), directed by Frank Launder
- *Lawrence of Arabia* (1962), directed by David Lean
- *Women in Love* (1969), directed by Ken Russell
- *Don't Look Now* (1973), directed by Nicolas Roeg
- *Chariots of Fire* (1981), directed by Hugh Hudson
- *The Killing Fields* (1984), directed by Roland Joffé
- *Four Weddings and a Funeral* (1994), directed by Mike Newell
- *Touching the Void* (2003), directed by Kevin MacDonald ⧉

Check your learning

4.31 Which of the following was famous for acting as a tramp in silent movies in the early days of cinema?

☐ Richard Burton ☐ Laurence Olivier
☐ David Niven ☐ Charlie Chaplin

⧉ British comedy

The traditions of comedy and <u>satire</u>, and the ability to laugh at ourselves, are an important part of the UK character.

Medieval kings and rich nobles had <u>jesters</u> who told jokes and made fun of people in the Court. Later, Shakespeare included comic characters in his plays. In the 18th century, political cartoons attacking prominent politicians – and, sometimes, the monarch or other members of the Royal Family – became increasingly popular. In the 19th century, satirical magazines began to be published. The most famous was *Punch*, which was published for the first time in the 1840s. Today, political cartoons continue to be published in newspapers, and magazines such as *Private Eye* continue the tradition of satire.

Comedians were a popular feature of British music hall, a form of variety theatre which was very common until television became the leading form of entertainment in the UK. Some of the people who had performed in the music halls in the 1940s and 1950s, such as Morecambe and Wise, became stars of television.

Television comedy developed its own style. Situation comedies, or sitcoms, which often look at family life and relationships in the workplace, remain popular. Satire has also continued to be important, with shows like *That Was the Week That Was* in the 1960s and *Spitting Image* in the 1980s and 1990s. In 1969, *Monty Python's Flying Circus* introduced a new type of progressive comedy. Stand-up comedy, where a solo comedian talks to a live audience, has become popular again in recent years. 🏴

Check your learning

4.32 Can you complete the following sentence?

Popular comedians from the music halls in the 1940s and 1950s became stars of _____.

🏴 Television and radio

Many different television (TV) channels are available in the UK. Some are free to watch and others require a paid subscription. British television shows a wide variety of programmes. Popular programmes include regular soap operas such as *Coronation Street* and *EastEnders*. In Scotland, some Scotland-specific programmes are shown and there is also a channel with programmes in the Gaelic language. There is a Welsh-language channel in Wales. There are also programmes specific to Northern Ireland and some programmes broadcast in Irish Gaelic.

Everyone in the UK with a TV, computer or other medium which can be used for watching TV must have a television <u>licence</u>. One licence covers all of the equipment in one home, except when people rent different rooms in a shared house and each has a separate <u>tenancy agreement</u> – these people must each buy a separate licence. People over 75 can apply for a free TV licence and blind people can get a 50% discount. You will receive a fine of up to £1,000 if you watch TV but do not have a TV licence.

The money from TV licences is used to pay for the British Broadcasting Corporation (BBC). This is a British public service broadcaster providing television and radio programmes. The BBC is the largest broadcaster in the world. It is the only wholly state-funded <u>media</u> organisation that is independent of government. Other UK channels are primarily funded through advertisements and subscriptions.

There are also many different radio stations in the UK. Some broadcast nationally and others in certain cities and regions. There are radio stations that play certain types of music and some broadcast in regional languages such as Welsh or Gaelic. Like television, BBC radio stations are funded by TV licences and other radio stations are funded through advertisements. 🇬🇧

🧠 Check your learning

4.33 Is the following statement **True** or **False**?

> People who only watch television on a computer at home do not have to buy a television licence.

🇬🇧 Social networking

Social networking websites such as Facebook and Twitter are a popular way for people to stay in touch with friends, organise social events, and share photos, videos and <u>opinions</u>. Many people use social networking on their mobile phones when out and about.

Pubs and night clubs

Public houses (pubs) are an important part of the UK social culture. Many people enjoy meeting friends in the pub. Most communities will have a 'local' pub that is a natural focal point for social activities. Pub quizzes are popular. Pool and darts are traditional pub games. To buy alcohol in a pub or night club you must be 18 or over, but people under that age may be allowed in some pubs with an adult. When they are 16, people can drink wine or beer with a meal in a hotel or restaurant (including eating areas in pubs) as long as they are with someone over 18.

© Zelfit / Shutterstock.com

Pubs are usually open during the day from 11.00 am (12 noon on Sundays). Night clubs with dancing and music usually open and close later than pubs. The <u>licensee</u> decides the hours that the pub or night club is open.

Dartboard

Betting and gambling

In the UK, people often enjoy a <u>gamble</u> on sports or other events. There are also casinos in many places. You have to be 18 to go into betting shops or gambling clubs. There is a National Lottery for which draws are made every week. You can enter by buying a ticket or a scratch card. People under 16 are not allowed to participate in the National Lottery. 🇬🇧

Check your learning

4.34 What age do you have to be to buy alcohol in a pub or go into a betting shop or gambling club?

☐ 16   ☐ 18   ☐ 21   ☐ 23

🇬🇧 Pets

A lot of people in the UK have pets such as cats or dogs. They might have them for company or because they enjoy looking after them. It is against the law to treat a pet cruelly or neglect it. All dogs in public places must wear a collar showing the name and address of the owner. The owner is responsible for keeping the dog under control and for cleaning up after the animal in a public place.

Vaccinations and medical treatment for animals are available from veterinary surgeons (vets). There are charities which may help people who cannot afford to pay a vet. 🇬🇧

🤔 Check your learning

4.35 Which of the following sentences is correct?

A   Any dog in a public place must wear a collar showing the name and address of its owner.

B   Any dog in a public place must wear a collar showing the name and address of its vet.

🇬🇧 Places of interest

The UK has a large network of public footpaths in the countryside. There are also many opportunities for mountain biking, mountaineering and hill walking. There are 15 national parks in England, Wales and Scotland. They are areas of protected countryside that everyone can visit, and where people live, work and look after the landscape.

There are many museums in the UK, which range from small community museums to large national and civic collections. Famous landmarks exist in towns, cities and the countryside throughout the UK. Most of them are open to the public to view (generally for a charge).

Many parts of the countryside and places of interest are kept open by the

National Trust in England, Wales and Northern Ireland and the National Trust for Scotland. Both are charities that work to preserve important buildings, coastline and countryside in the UK. The National Trust was founded in 1895 by three volunteers. There are now more than 61,000 volunteers helping to keep the organisation running. 🇬🇧

Natural History Museum, London

Check your learning

4.36 What is the name of the charity that looks after important buildings, coastlines and countryside in England, Wales and Northern Ireland?

🇬🇧 UK landmarks

Big Ben

Big Ben is the nickname for the great bell of the clock at the Houses of Parliament in London. Many people call the clock Big Ben as well. The clock is over 150 years old and is a popular tourist attraction. The clock tower is named 'Elizabeth Tower' in honour of Queen Elizabeth II's Diamond Jubilee in 2012.

The Eden Project

© Alexandra Thompson / Shutterstock.com

The Eden Project is located in Cornwall, in the south west of England. Its biomes, like giant greenhouses, house plants from all over the world. The Eden Project is also a charity which runs <u>environmental</u> and social projects internationally.

Edinburgh Castle

© StockCube / Shutterstock.com

The Castle is a <u>dominant</u> feature of the skyline in Edinburgh, Scotland. It has a long history, dating back to the early Middle Ages. It is looked after by Historic Scotland, a Scottish <u>government agency</u>.

The Giant's Causeway

© Paul Krugman / Shutterstock.com

Located on the north-east coast of Northern Ireland, the Giant's Causeway is a land formation of columns made from <u>volcanic lava</u>. It was formed about 50 million years ago. There are many <u>legends</u> about the Causeway and how it was formed.

Loch Lomond and the Trossachs National Park

© Tamara Kulikova / Shutterstock.com

This park covers 720 square miles (1,865 square kilometres) in the west of Scotland. Loch Lomond is the largest expanse of fresh water in mainland Britain and probably the best known part of the park.

London Eye

The London Eye is situated on the southern bank of the River Thames and is a <u>Ferris wheel</u> that is 443 feet (135 metres) tall. It was originally built as part of the UK's celebration of the new <u>millennium</u> and continues to be an important part of New Year celebrations.

© JLRphotography / Shutterstock.com

Snowdonia

© Collpicto / Shutterstock.com

Snowdonia is a national park in North Wales. It covers an area of 838 square miles (2,170 square kilometres). Its most well-known landmark is Snowdon, which is the highest mountain in Wales.

The Tower of London

© Mapics / Shutterstock.com

The Tower of London was first built by William the Conqueror after he became king in 1066. Tours are given by the Yeoman Warders, also known as Beefeaters, who tell visitors about the building's history. People can also see the Crown Jewels there.

The Lake District

© Mapics / Shutterstock.com

The Lake District is England's largest national park. It covers 885 square miles (2,292 square kilometres). It is famous for its lakes and mountains and is very popular with climbers, walkers and sailors. The biggest stretch of water is Windermere. In 2007, television viewers voted Wastwater as Britain's favourite view. 🇬🇧

Check your learning

4.37 Without looking at the text, fill in the table below to help you remember the most important information about UK landmarks and places of interest. Then check your answers by looking at the text on pages 206–207. We have started it for you:

Landmark or Place	Where it is	Notes
Big Ben	London, England	Name of the clock bell at the Houses of Parliament 150 years old Tower called 'Elizabeth Tower' for the Queen's Diamond Jubilee in 2012
Eden Project	_____	Giant greenhouses called biomes Plants from all over the world
_____ Castle	Scotland	
_____	North-east coast of Northern Ireland	Columns made from volcanic lava 50 million years ago
Loch Lomond and the Trossachs	_____	
_____ Eye	_____	
_____	North Wales	National park _____ – highest mountain in Wales
_____	London	Tower built by William the Conqueror
Lake District	_____	

Check your understanding

Now that you have read Section 6, what can you remember about the following?

- What people in the UK like to do in their free time
- Traditional foods that people eat in the four nations of the UK
- The development of the British film industry
- British comedy, television and radio
- The television licence and how it is used to pay for the BBC
- Some interesting buildings and places of natural beauty to visit in the UK

Revision questions and end of chapter checklist

You have completed Chapter Four. Now that you have read the study materials, checked your learning and done a few tasks, try to answer the following revision questions. If you are not sure of the answers, use your notes or look back at the study material before checking the answers at the end of the chapter.

1   What is the currency used in the UK called?

    Answer:
    _____

2   Which country in the UK has the smallest population?

    Answer:
    _____

3   Are employers allowed to ask women to leave their job when they get married or have children?

    Answer:
    _____

4   Of which country is St David the patron saint?

Answer:

_____

5   Who is the spiritual leader of the Church of England?

Answer:

_____

6   In what year did both the Olympic and Paralympic Games take place in the UK?

Answer:

_____

7   What is the UK's most popular sport?

Answer

_____

8   Where does a series of arts and cultural festivals, the biggest of which is the Fringe Festival, take place?

Answer:

_____

9   What does the Turner Prize celebrate?

Answer

_____

10 Name a famous cathedral that the architect Sir Christopher Wren designed.

Answer:

11 For what is the Man Booker Prize awarded every year?

Answer:

12 Up to how much can you be fined for owning and watching television in your home without buying a licence?

Answer:

13 At what age can a young person buy a lottery ticket?

Answer:

14 Where can you see the Eden Project?

Answer:

End of Chapter Four checklist

Now that you have come to the end of Chapter Four, tick the boxes when you have:

- read the study material ☐
- made short notes, drawings and timelines to help you with your revision ☐
- looked up words that you do not understand and made a note of them ☐
- completed the 'Check your learning' and revision questions and checked your answers ☐
- read the study material again for the questions you got wrong ☐

Glossary

allotment	A small piece of land that people can rent for growing vegetables, fruits or flowers.
animation	Technique for using drawings to create movement for a film; for example, cartoons.
anniversary	The date on which something happened in a previous year. Your birthday is the anniversary of your birth.
associated	Connected, linked.
award	A prize or reward for doing something special.
Cenotaph	A monument built in memory of the people who died in war.
chairperson	Someone who controls a meeting or an organisation.
character	(here) People created by a writer in a book, play or film.
charity	An organisation that raises money, usually to give help to those who need it or for a particular purpose, for example; for medical research, art or historic buildings.
choir	A group of people who sing together, particularly in a church.

civic collection	A collection by a town or city council; for example, objects in a city museum or art gallery.
comedian	Someone who tells jokes and makes funny shows.
comic opera	A funny play with lots of music and singing that ends happily.
commercially successful	Made a profit.
composer	Person who writes music.
constitutional	Related to the constitution.
descent	(here) With parents or grandparents who came from a particular country, race or culture.
dialect	A form of language spoken by a particular group or people living in a particular area.
discrimination	Treating someone, or a group of people, in a certain way, particularly in a bad way, because of their colour, race, gender, sexuality, disability or other difference.
diverse population	A nation made up of people from many different backgrounds, classes, cultures, races, religions and beliefs.
dominant	Most important; standing out.
environmental	Related to the air, water and land where people, animals and plants live.
ethnic	Related to a race or nationality.
expressions	Sayings or phrases that have special meanings.
fair play	To do something in a fair and honest way.
featuring	Including someone or something as an important part.
Ferris wheel	A huge wheel that turns slowly in which people can ride.
fiction	Made up stories, people or events.
film franchise	A series of films with the same main characters and type of story; for example, James Bond, Star Wars or Harry Potter.
gamble	To bet money on the result of something - for example, a game, competition or race.

gothic	A style of building developed in Europe between the 12th and 16th centuries which became popular in the 19th century.
government agency	An organisation that the government gives responsibility for a particular task; for example, health and safety.
heritage	Customs, buildings, art, etc. which are important in a culture or society because they have existed for a long time.
highest-grossing	Made the most money.
household chores	Tasks that are done around the house, such as cleaning or cooking.
hymn	Religious song usually sung in Christian churches.
idiosyncratic	A particular way of behaving that other people may find strange.
illustration	Drawing, painting, photograph or other image that accompanies text.
innovate	Introduce new ideas and changes.
jester	Person in medieval times whose job it was to make people laugh.
landmark	A feature that is easy recognisable, such as a monument, building or other structure.
landscape	An area of countryside or a painting of the countryside.
legend	An old story from the past.
licence	An official document that allows you to do or have something.
licensee	Person with permission to sell alcoholic drinks.
light-hearted	Cheerful and not serious.
media	Magazines, newspapers, radio, television or other forms of communication.
migration	Movement from one country to another.

millennium	A period of 1,000 years; here the millennium means the year 2000.
multinational	Involving different countries.
multiracial	Involving people of different races.
national parks	Large areas of the countryside that are protected by law for the public.
novelist	Someone who writes books about imagined peoples and stories.
opinions	Beliefs or values about a particular subject.
oratorio	A piece of music for an orchestra and singers that tells a story, usually on a religious subject.
orchestral classical	Traditional music by great composers such as Mozart or Beethoven played by a large group of musicians with different musical instruments, such as violins, cellos, flutes, clarinets, etc.
organist	Someone who plays an organ, a musical instrument like a piano that produces different notes when air is blown through pipes.
originated	Began.
ornate	Decorated with complicated patterns.
Pagan	(here) Religion in the UK before Christianity, which included worshipping nature.
pantomime	Funny play performed around Christmas, based on traditional children's stories.
Premier League	A group of the 20 top football clubs in England.
prestigious	Very important, admired and respected.
progressive comedy	New and different comedy that can shock people with traditional tastes.
publish	(here) Print something for sale.
references	(here) Mentions someone or something.
rivalry	Competing with another person or people.

saint	A person recognised by a religion for their goodness.
satire	Using jokes and humour to criticise people or ideas; making fun of people or ideas to criticise them.
slaughterhouse	Place where animals are killed for their meat.
soap operas	Series of television or radio programmes that tell the story of a group of characters over a long period of time.
special effects	Action in a film, or entertainment on stage, created by using special equipment or computers.
spiritual leader	Person responsible for religious matters and beliefs.
subscription	An amount of money that you pay regularly to receive a product or service or to be a member of an organisation.
tenancy agreement	A contract between someone renting a place to live (a tenant) and whoever who owns the property.
tournament	A competition with a series of games between many teams or players, with one winner at the end.
vaccination	To give someone a substance to stop them from getting a disease.
volcanic lava	Hot liquid rock that is forced out from the earth in a huge explosion that cools and becomes solid over time.
volunteering	Working without pay.
wreath	A ring of leaves and flowers.

Answers to 'Check your learning' questions

4.1   B   Nearly 10% of the population has a parent or grandparent born outside the UK.

4.2   England   London
          Northern Ireland   Belfast
          Scotland   Edinburgh
          Wales   Cardiff

4.3   £5, £10, £20, £50

4.4   Welsh, Gaelic, Irish Gaelic

4.5   True

4.6   England 84%, Wales 5%, Scotland just over 8%, Northern Ireland just under 3%

4.7   ✓ White

4.8   False

4.9   B 21% of people said they had no religion
       C 4% of people said they were Muslim

4.10 The Church of Scotland is a <u>Presbyterian</u> Church.

4.11 False

4.12

The birth of Jesus Christ	B	Christmas
The death of Jesus Christ	C	Good Friday
Jesus Christ rising from the dead	A	Easter

4.13 Hindu C   Jewish D   Muslim A   Sikh B

4.14 ✓ St Valentine's Day

4.15 False

4.16 ✓ B Cardiff

4.17 False

4.18

Bradley Wiggins	Running
Ellie Simmonds	Cycling
Mo Farah	Rowing
Sir Steve Redgrave	Swimming

4.19 Tick the boxes beside the three sports in the list below that began in Britain:

       ✓ Cricket   ✓ Golf   ✓ Lawn Tennis

4.20   George Frederic Handel   Water Music
Gustav Holst   The Planets
Edward Elgar   Land of Hope and Glory
Benjamin Britten   Young Person's Guide to the
Orchestra

4.21   Beatles or Rolling Stones

4.22   ✓ The Mousetrap

4.23   Every summer a number of arts and cultural festivals are held in
Edinburgh, with the biggest being the Edinburgh **Fringe** Festival.

4.24   ✓ David Allan   ✓ Thomas Gainsborough

4.25   A The Queen's House at Greenwich
B St Paul's Cathedral in London
C Dumfries House in Scotland
D The Cenotaph in London

4.26   ✓ Gertrude Jekyll

4.27   B

4.28   A *Pride and Prejudice*
B *Treasure Island, Dr Jekyll and Mr Hyde*
C Sherlock Holmes stories
D Harry Potter books

4.29   Wilfred Owen or Siegfried Sassoon

4.30

Country	Wales	England	Northern Ireland	Scotland
National flower or plant	Daffodil	Rose	Shamrock	Thistle
Traditional food	Welsh cakes	Roast beef and Yorkshire pudding	Ulster fry	Haggis

4.31 ✓ Charlie Chaplin

4.32 Popular comedians from the music halls in the 1940s and 1950s became stars of <u>television</u>.

4.33 False

4.34 18

4.36 A Any dog in a public place must wear a collar showing the name and address of its owner.

4.36 National Trust

4.37 Landmarks

Big Ben	London, England
Eden Project	**Cornwall**
Edinburgh Castle	**Edinburgh,** Scotland
Giant's Causeway	North-east coast of Northern Ireland
Loch Lomond and the Trossachs	**Scotland/west of Scotland**
London Eye	**London, England**
Snowdonia	North Wales, Snowdon – highest mountain in Wales
Tower of London	London, England
Lake District	**England**

Answers to revision questions

1 Sterling or pounds sterling
2 Northern Ireland
3 No
4 Wales
5 Archbishop of Canterbury
6 2012
7 Football
8 Edinburgh
9 Contemporary art or art
10 St Paul's
11 Best novel or best fiction novel
12 £1000
13 16
14 Cornwall

CHAPTER FIVE

The UK government, the law and your role

In this chapter you will read the official study material about the development of democratic government in the UK, its traditions and the many different organisations that make up this system. It describes the relationships between the UK and international organisations, aspects of the law and explores your role in the community and in the democratic process.

This chapter is divided into the following sections:

Section 1 The development of British democracy

Section 2 The British constitution

Section 3 The government

Section 4 Voting

Section 5 The UK and international institutions

Section 6 Respecting the law

Section 7 The role of the courts

Section 8 Fundamental principles

Section 9 Your role in the community

SECTION 1 The development of British democracy

The UK is a parliamentary democracy with the monarch as head of state. This section will tell you about the different <u>institutions</u> which make up this democratic system and explain how you can play a part in the democratic system.

The development of British democracy

Democracy is a system of government where the whole adult population gets a say. This might be by direct voting or by choosing representatives to make decisions on their behalf.

At the turn of the 19th century, Britain was not a democracy as we know it today. Although there were elections to select members of Parliament (MPs), only a small number of people could vote. They were men who were over 21 years of age and who owned a certain amount of property.

The franchise (that is, the number of people who had the right to vote) grew over the course of the 19th century and political parties began to involve ordinary men and women as members.

In the 1830s and 1840s, a group called the Chartists campaigned for reform. They wanted six changes:

- for every man to have the vote
- elections every year
- for all regions to be equal in the electoral system
- <u>secret ballots</u>
- for any man to be able to stand as an MP
- for MPs to be paid.

At the time, the campaign was generally seen as a failure. However, by 1918 most of these reforms had been <u>adopted</u>. The voting <u>franchise</u> was also extended to women over 30, and then in 1928 to men and women over 21. In 1969, the voting age was reduced to 18 for men and women.

Chartists petitioning Parliament

Check your learning

5.1 Is the statement below **True** or **False**?

At the beginning of the 1800s, all men over the age of 30 could vote for Members of Parliament.

5.2 From what age can people in the UK vote today?

☐ 16   ☐ 18   ☐ 20   ☐ 21

Find out more

Until 1872, men who had the vote had to tell an official the name of the person they were voting for. The official wrote it in a book. This was all done in public so everyone could hear. Voters could be bribed or pressured to vote for particular candidates until the Ballot Act brought in the secret system of voting that we use today.

Check your understanding

Now that you have finished Section 1, what do you remember about the following?

■ The development of democracy in the UK

■ When different groups of people were able to vote

SECTION 2 The British constitution

In this section you will read about the following:

- **the institutions or different parts of the government**
- **the monarchy**
- **the system of government**
- **the House of Commons**
- **the House of Lords**
- **the Speaker's role**
- **elections in the UK**
- **how to contact your government representatives**

A constitution is a set of principles by which a country is governed. It includes all of the institutions that are responsible for running the country and how their power is <u>kept in check</u>. The constitution also includes laws and <u>conventions</u>. The British constitution is not written down in any single document, and therefore it is described as 'unwritten'. This is mainly because the UK, unlike America or France, has never had a revolution which led permanently to a totally new system of government. Our most important institutions have developed over hundreds of years. Some people believe that there should be a single document, but others believe an unwritten constitution allows for more flexibility and better government.

Constitutional institutions

In the UK, there are several different parts of government. The main ones are:

- the monarchy
- Parliament (the House of Commons and the House of Lords)
- the Prime Minister

- the judiciary (law courts)
- the police
- the <u>civil service</u>
- local government.

In addition, there are <u>devolved</u> governments in Scotland, Wales and Northern Ireland that have the power to <u>legislate</u> on certain issues.

 Check your learning

5.3 Without looking at the text, can you name three of the main parts of government?

1. _____

2. _____

3. _____

The monarchy

© Shaun Jeffers / Shutterstock.com

Queen Elizabeth II is the head of state of the UK. She is also the monarch or head of state for many countries in the Commonwealth. The UK has a constitutional monarchy. This means that the king or queen does not rule the country but appoints the government, which the people have chosen in a democratic election. The monarch invites the leader of the party with the largest number of MPs, or the leader of a coalition between more than one party, to become the Prime Minister. The monarch has regular meetings with the Prime Minister and can advise, warn and encourage, but the decisions on government policies are made by the Prime Minister and cabinet (see the next section on 'The government').

The Queen has reigned since her father's death in 1952, and in 2012 she celebrated her Diamond Jubilee (60 years as queen). She is married to Prince Philip, the Duke of Edinburgh. Her eldest son, Prince Charles (the Prince of Wales), is the <u>heir to the throne</u>.

The Queen has important ceremonial roles, such as the opening of the new parliamentary session each year. On this occasion the Queen makes a speech which summarises the government's policies for the year ahead. All Acts of Parliament are made in her name.

The Queen represents the UK to the rest of the world. She receives foreign ambassadors and high commissioners, <u>entertains</u> visiting heads of state, and makes state visits overseas in support of diplomatic and economic relationships with other countries.

The Queen has an important role in providing <u>stability</u> and <u>continuity</u>. While governments and Prime Ministers change regularly, the Queen continues as head of state. She provides a focus for national identity and pride, which was demonstrated through the celebrations of her Jubilee.

The National Anthem

The National Anthem of the UK is 'God Save the Queen'. It is played at important national occasions and at events attended by the Queen or the Royal Family. The first verse is:

God save our gracious Queen!
Long live our noble Queen!
God save the Queen!
Send her victorious,
Happy and glorious,
Long to reign over us,
God save the Queen!

New citizens swear or affirm loyalty to the Queen as part of the citizenship ceremony.

Oath of allegiance

I (name) swear by Almighty God that on becoming a British citizen, I will be faithful and bear true allegiance to Her Majesty Queen Elizabeth the Second, her Heirs and Successors, according to law.

Affirmation of allegiance

I (name) do solemnly, sincerely and truly declare and affirm that on becoming a British citizen, I will be faithful and bear true <u>allegiance</u> to Her Majesty Queen Elizabeth the Second, her Heirs and Successors, according to law.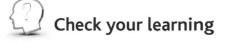

Check your learning

5.4 Which of the following is the head of state of the UK?

  ☐ A   The Prime Minister   ☐ B   Queen Elizabeth II

  ☐ C   Prince Charles   ☐ D   Prince Philip

 System of government

The system of government in the UK is a parliamentary democracy. The UK is divided into parliamentary constituencies. Voters in each <u>constituency</u> elect their Member of Parliament (MP) in a General Election. All of the elected MPs form the House of Commons. Most MPs belong to a political party, and the party with the majority of MPs forms the government. If one party does not get a majority, two parties can join together to form a coalition.

The House of Commons

The House of Commons is regarded as the more important of the two chambers in Parliament because its members are democratically elected. The Prime Minister and almost all the members of the cabinet are members of the House of Commons (MPs). Each MP represents a parliamentary constituency, which is a small area of the country. MPs have a number of different responsibilities. They:

- represent everyone in their constituency
- help to create new laws
- <u>scrutinise</u> and comment on what the government is doing
- <u>debate</u> national issues.

Find out more

The House of Lords has red carpets and leather benches, and the House of Commons has green carpets and leather benches.

In the House of Commons, the Prime Minister and ministers sit facing the Leader of the Opposition and senior opposition MPs on the front benches. Other MPs sit at the back of them. You sometimes hear MPs being called frontbenchers and backbenchers.

⊞ The House of Lords

Members of the House of Lords, known as peers, are not elected by the people and do not represent a constituency. The role and membership of the House of Lords has changed over the last 50 years.

Until 1958, all peers were:

■ 'hereditary', which means they <u>inherited</u> their title, or

■ senior judges, or

■ bishops of the Church of England.

Since 1958, the Prime Minister has had the power to <u>nominate</u> peers just for their own lifetime. These are called life peers. They have usually had an important career in politics, business, law or another profession. Life peers are appointed by the monarch on the advice of the Prime Minister. They also include people nominated by the leaders of the other main political parties or by an independent Appointments Commission for non-party peers.

Since 1999, hereditary peers have lost the automatic right to attend the House of Lords. They now elect a few of their number to represent them in the House of Lords.

The House of Lords is normally more independent of the government than the House of Commons. It can suggest <u>amendments</u> or propose new laws, which are then discussed by MPs. The House of Lords checks laws that have been passed by the House of Commons to ensure they are <u>fit for purpose</u>. It also holds the government to account to make sure that it is working in the best interests of the people. There are peers who are specialists in particular areas, and their knowledge is useful in making and checking laws. The House of Commons has powers to <u>overrule</u> the House of Lords, but these are not used often.

The Speaker

Debates in the House of Commons are chaired by the <u>Speaker</u>. This person is the chief officer of the House of Commons. The Speaker is neutral and does not represent a political party, even though he or she is an MP, represents a constituency and deals with constituents' problems like any other MP. The Speaker is chosen by other MPs in a secret ballot.

The Speaker keeps order during political debates to make sure the rules are followed. This includes making sure the opposition (see the section on 'The government') has a guaranteed amount of time to debate issues which it chooses. The Speaker also represents Parliament on ceremonial occasions.

Check your learning

5.5 Which of the following statements is correct?

☐ A The House of Commons is regarded as the more important of the two chambers in Parliament.

☐ B The House of Lords is regarded as the more important of the two chambers in Parliament.

5.6 Look at the list on the next page and match the roles to the correct definitions. We have done one as an example. You may want to use this to help you with your revision later.

British Parliamentary System

1. MPs	A Appointed by the Queen to the House of Lords on the advice of the Prime Minister
2. Leader of the Opposition	B Committee of ministers who make decisions about government policy
3. Life Peers	C Leader of the political party in power
4. Speaker	D Makes sure that rules of debate are followed in the House of Commons
5. Prime Minister	E Leader of the second largest party in the House of Commons
6. Members of the Cabinet	F Members of Parliament elected by the voters in their constituency

Find out more

Many peers have led reforms that later became laws. For example, Lord Ashley, who was made a Labour peer in 1992 and was deaf himself, persuaded Parliament to pass a law that gave equal rights for people with disabilities.

🇬🇧 Elections

UK elections

MPs are elected at a General Election, which is held at least every five years. If an MP dies or resigns, there will be a fresh election, called a <u>by-election</u>, in his or her constituency.

MPs are elected through a system called 'first past the post'. In each constituency the candidate who gets the most votes is elected. The government is usually formed by the party that wins the majority of constituencies. If no party wins a majority, two parties may join together to a form a <u>coalition</u>.

European parliamentary elections

Elections for the European Parliament are also held every five years. Elected members are called members of the European Parliament (MEPs). Elections to the European Parliament use a system of <u>proportional representation</u>, where seats are allocated to each party in <u>proportion</u> to the total number of votes it has won.

Contacting elected members

All elected members have a duty to serve and represent their constituents. You can get contact details for all your representatives and their parties from your local library and from www.parliament.uk. MPs, Assembly members, members of the Scottish Parliament (MSPs) and MEPs are also listed in _The Phone Book_, published by BT, and in the _Yellow Pages_.

You can contact MPs by letter or telephone at their constituency office, or at their office in the House of Commons: The House of Commons, Westminster, London SW1A 0AA, telephone 020 7729 3000. In addition, many MPs, Assembly members, MSPs and MEPs hold regular local 'surgeries', where constituents can go in person to talk about issues that are of concern to them. These surgeries are often advertised in the local newspaper.

Check your learning

5.7 Complete the following sentence with one of the options below:

General Elections and elections for the European Parliament are held at least every

A ☐ 4 years   B ☐ 5 years   C ☐ 6 years   D ☐ 7 years

5.8 Is the following statement **True** or **False**?

The only way to contact your MP is to write to him or her at the House of Commons.

Check your understanding

Now that you have finished Section 2, look at the checklist below and write down brief notes about the following:

- The development of democracy in the UK
- When different groups of people were able to vote
- What a constitution is and how the UK's constitution is different from that of many other countries
- The role of the monarch
- The roles of the House of Commons and the House of Lords
- What the Speaker does
- The different types of representatives: MPs, MEPs, MSPs and Assembly Members

SECTION 3 The government

In this section you will read about the following:

- **the Prime Minister**
- **the cabinet**
- **the opposition**
- **the party system**
- **the civil service**
- **local government**
- **devolved administrations**
- **the media and government**

⊞ The Prime Minister

The Prime Minister (PM) is the leader of the political party in power. He or she appoints the members of the cabinet (see below) and has control over many important <u>public appointments</u>. The official home of the Prime Minister is 10 Downing Street. He or she also has a country house outside London called Chequers.

The Prime Minister can be changed if the MPs in the governing party decide to do so, or if he or she wishes to resign. The Prime Minister usually resigns if his or her party loses a General Election.

The cabinet

The Prime Minister appoints about 20 senior MPs to become ministers in charge of <u>departments</u>. These include:

- Chancellor of the Exchequer – responsible for the economy
- Home Secretary – responsible for crime, policing and immigration

- Foreign Secretary – responsible for managing relationships with foreign countries

- other ministers (called 'Secretaries of State') – responsible for subjects such as education, health and defence.

The ministers form the cabinet, a <u>committee</u> which usually meets weekly and makes important decisions about government <u>policy</u>. Many of these decisions have to be debated or approved by Parliament.

Each department also has a number of other ministers, called Ministers of State and Parliamentary Under-Secretaries of State, who take charge of particular areas of the department's work.

Check your learning

5.9 Can you match the titles of the ministers with their responsibilities? We have done one for you:

A Foreign Secretary	responsible for policing and immigration
B Chancellor of the Exchequer	responsible for managing relationships with foreign countries
C Home Secretary	responsible for schools, colleges and universities
D Secretary of State for Education	responsible for the economy

Find out more

The title of Chancellor of the Exchequer is very old and was first mentioned at the time of the Norman kings. According to a medieval document it got its name from the French name for a special checked cloth on which the Chancellor counted out the money paid to the king in tax and rents. The Chancellor of the Exchequer is the equivalent of Ministers of Finance in other countries and is responsible for setting the budget for government spending every year.

🇬🇧 The opposition

The second-largest party in the House of Commons is called the <u>opposition</u>. The leader of the opposition usually becomes Prime Minister if his or her party wins the next General Election.

The leader of the opposition leads his or her party in pointing out what they see as the government's failures and weaknesses. One important opportunity to do this is at Prime Minister's Questions, which takes place every week while Parliament is sitting. The leader of the opposition also appoints senior opposition MPs to be 'shadow ministers'. They form the <u>shadow cabinet</u> and their role is to challenge the government and put forward alternative policies.

The party system

Anyone aged 18 or over can stand for election as an MP but they are unlikely to win unless they have been nominated to represent one of the major political parties. These are the Conservative Party, the Labour Party, the Liberal Democrats, or one of the parties representing Scottish, Welsh or Northern Irish interests.

There are a few MPs who do not represent any of the main political parties. They are called 'independents' and usually represent an issue important to their constituency.

The main political parties actively look for members of the public to join their debates, contribute to their costs, and help at elections for Parliament or for local government. They have branches in most constituencies and hold policy-making conferences every year.

Pressure and lobby groups are organisations which try to influence government policy. They play an important role in politics. Some are representative organisations such as the CBI (Confederation of British Industry), which represents the view of British business. Others campaign on particular topics, such as the environment (for example, Greenpeace) or human rights (for example, Liberty). 🇬🇧

Check your learning

5.10 Look at the list below and decide which ones are political parties and which ones are lobby groups. Write them in the table below under the correct heading. We have done one for you:

Conservatives   Greenpeace   CBI   Labour   Liberty   Liberal Democrats

Political party	Lobby group
	Liberty

The civil service

Civil servants support the government in developing and <u>implementing</u> its policies. They also deliver public services. Civil servants are <u>accountable</u> to ministers. They are <u>chosen on merit</u> and are <u>politically neutral</u> – they are not political appointees. People can apply to join the civil service through an application process, like other jobs in the UK. Civil servants are expected to carry out their role with dedication and a commitment to the civil service and its core values. These are: <u>integrity</u>, honesty, <u>objectivity</u> and <u>impartiality</u> (including being politically neutral).

Check your learning

5.11   Which of the following statements is correct?

A Jobs in the civil service are open to everyone and you have to go through an application process.

B Jobs in the civil service are only open to members of political parties and you have to be selected by an MP.

🇬🇧 Local government

Democratically elected councils, often called 'local authorities', govern towns, cities and <u>rural</u> areas in the UK. Some areas have both district and county councils, which have different <u>functions</u>. Most large towns and cities have a single local authority.

Local authorities provide a range of services in their areas. They are funded by money from central government and by local taxes.

Many local authorities appoint a mayor, who is the ceremonial leader of the council. In some towns, a mayor is elected to be the effective leader of the <u>administration</u>. London has 33 local authorities, with the Greater London Authority and the Mayor of London coordinating policies across the capital. For most local authorities, local elections for councillors are held in May every year. Many candidates stand for council election as members of a political party. 🇬🇧

Check your learning

5.12 What is the ceremonial leader of a local authority called?

🇬🇧 Devolved administrations

Since 1997, some powers have been devolved from the central government to give people in Wales, Scotland and Northern Ireland more control over matters that directly affect them. There has been a Welsh Assembly and a Scottish Parliament since 1999. There is also a Northern Ireland Assembly, although this has been <u>suspended</u> on a few occasions.

The devolved administrations each have their own civil service.

The Welsh government

The Welsh government and National Assembly for Wales are based in Cardiff, the capital city of Wales. The National Assembly has 60 Assembly members

(AMs) and elections are held every four years using a form of proportional representation. Members can speak in either Welsh or English, and all of the Assembly's publications are in both languages.

The Assembly has the power to make laws for Wales in 20 areas, including:

- education and training
- health and social services
- economic development
- housing.

Since 2011, the National Assembly for Wales has been able to pass laws on these topics without the agreement of the UK Parliament.

The Scottish Parliament

The Scottish Parliament was formed in 1999. It sits in Edinburgh, the capital city of Scotland.

There are 129 members of the Scottish Parliament (MSPs), elected by a form of proportional representation. The Scottish Parliament can pass laws for Scotland on all matters which are not specifically reserved to the UK Parliament. The matters on which the Scottish Parliament can legislate include:

- civil and criminal law
- health
- education
- planning
- additional tax-raising powers.

The Northern Ireland Assembly

The Northern Ireland Parliament was established in 1922, when Ireland was divided, but was <u>abolished</u> in 1972, shortly after the Troubles broke out in 1969 (see page 108).

The Northern Ireland Assembly was established soon after the Belfast Agreement (or Good Friday Agreement) in 1998. There is a power-sharing agreement which distributes ministerial offices amongst the main parties. The Assembly has 108 elected members, known as MLAs (members of the Legislative Assembly). They are elected with a form of proportional representation.

The Northern Ireland Assembly can make decisions on issues such as:

- education
- agriculture
- the environment
- health
- social services.

The UK government has the power to suspend all devolved assemblies. It has used this power several times in Northern Ireland when local political leaders found it difficult to work together. However, the Assembly has been running successfully since 2007.

Check your learning

5.13 Can you write down the names of the devolved governments where the following are members?

Members of the Legislative Assembly (MLAs)

_____

Assembly Members (AMs)

_____

5.14 What are the members of the third devolved government called?

_____

Study tip

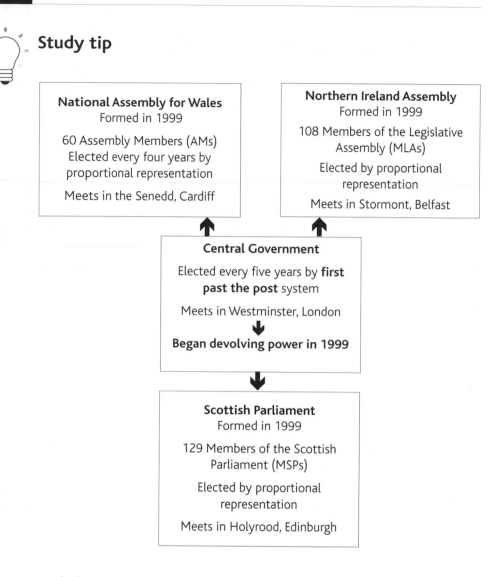

National Assembly for Wales
Formed in 1999

60 Assembly Members (AMs)
Elected every four years by
proportional representation

Meets in the Senedd, Cardiff

Northern Ireland Assembly
Formed in 1999

108 Members of the Legislative
Assembly (MLAs)

Elected by proportional
representation

Meets in Stormont, Belfast

Central Government

Elected every five years by **first
past the post** system

Meets in Westminster, London

Began devolving power in 1999

Scottish Parliament
Formed in 1999

129 Members of the Scottish
Parliament (MSPs)

Elected by proportional
representation

Meets in Holyrood, Edinburgh

Diagram to help you remember information about the UK central
government and the devolved administrations.

⊞ The media and government

Proceedings in Parliament are broadcast on television and published in official reports called Hansard. Written reports can be found in large libraries and at www.parliament.uk. Most people get information about political issues and events from newspapers (often called 'the press'), television, radio and the internet.

The UK has a free press. This means that what is written in newspapers is free from government control. Some newspaper owners and editors hold strong political opinions and run campaigns to try to influence government policy and public opinion.

By law, radio and television <u>coverage</u> of the political parties must be balanced and so equal time has to be given to <u>rival viewpoints.</u> ⊞

⌢ Check your learning

5.15 Which of the following statements is correct?

   A The UK has a free press, which means that the government **cannot** tell newspapers what they can or cannot write.

   B The UK does not have a free press, which means that the government **can** tell newspapers what they can or cannot write.

Find out more

The Sun newspaper was accused of being 'tasteless and wrong' for using the headline 'It's The Sun Wot Won It' after supporting former Prime Minister John Major's election campaign.

Find out more

Although the UK government cannot tell the press what to report, there are some things the press cannot say. Judges can forbid them to make certain information public and they can be taken to court if they say anything that is not true.

Study tip

Using the information below, make a diagram to help you remember the different parts of the British Constitution. Follow the example on page 240.

The Structure of the British Constitution

The Monarchy

Parliament
      House of Commons
      House of Lords

Prime Minister   Leader of the Opposition
Cabinet   Shadow Cabinet
Judiciary
Police
Civil Service
Local Government

Devolved administrations
      Welsh Assembly
      Northern Ireland Assembly
      Parliament of Scotland

Check your understanding

Now that you have finished Section 3, what do you remember about the following? You could write down brief notes about each one or explain what you have learnt to someone else.

- The role of the Prime Minister, cabinet, opposition and shadow cabinet
- The role of political parties in the UK system of government
- Who the main political parties are
- What pressure and lobby groups do
- The role of the civil service
- The role of local government
- The powers of the devolved governments in Wales, Scotland and Northern Ireland
- Where you can watch or read about the proceedings in Parliament
- Media reporting of political issues

SECTION 4 Voting

In this section you will read about the following:

- who is allowed to vote
- how you register to vote
- where to vote in the different parts of the UK
- who can stand for public office
- how you can arrange to visit Parliament, the Northern Ireland Assembly, the Scottish Parliament and the Welsh Assembly

Who can vote?

The UK has had a fully democratic voting system since 1928 (see pages 222–223). The present voting age of 18 was set in 1969 and (with a few exceptions) all UK-born and naturalised adult citizens have the right to vote.

Adult citizens of the UK, and citizens of the Commonwealth and the Irish Republic who are resident in the UK, can vote in all public elections. Adult citizens of other EU states who are resident in the UK can vote in all elections except General Elections.

The electoral register

To be able to vote in a parliamentary, local or European election, you must have your name on the electoral register.

If you are eligible to vote, you can register by contacting your local council electoral registration office. This is usually based at your local council (in Scotland it may be based elsewhere). If you do not know which local authority you come under, you can find out by visiting www.aboutmyvote.co.uk and entering your postcode. You can also download voter registration forms in English, Welsh and some other languages.

The electoral register is updated every year in September or October. An electoral registration form is sent to every household and this has to be completed and returned with the names of everyone who is resident in the household and eligible to vote.

In Northern Ireland a different system operates. This is called 'individual registration' and all those entitled to vote must complete their own registration form. Once registered, people stay on the register provided their personal details do not change. For more information see the Electoral Office for Northern Ireland website at www.eoni.org.uk.

By law, each local authority has to make its electoral register available for anyone to look at, although this has to be supervised. The register is kept at each local electoral registration office (or council office in England and Wales). It is also possible to see the register at some public buildings such as libraries.

Check your learning

5.16 Which of the following statements is correct?

A If you are over 18 and from a country in the European Union and resident in the UK, you can vote in a General Election.

B If you are over 18 and a Commonwealth citizen and resident in the UK, you can vote in a General Election.

Where to vote

People vote in elections at places called polling stations, or polling places in Scotland. Before the election you will be sent a poll card. This tells you where your polling station or polling place is and when the election will take place. On election day, the polling station or place will be open from 7.00 am until 10.00 pm.

When you arrive at the polling station, the staff will ask for your name and address. In Northern Ireland you will also have to show photographic identification. You will then get your ballot paper, which you take to a polling booth to fill in privately. You should make up your own mind who to

© secretlondon123 / Flickr

vote for. No one has the right to make you vote for a particular candidate. You should follow the instructions on the ballot paper. Once you have completed it, put it in the ballot box.

If it is difficult for you to get to a polling station or polling place, you can register for a postal ballot. Your ballot paper will be sent to your home before the election. You then fill it in and post it back. You can register to do this when you register to vote. 🇬🇧

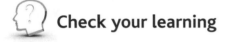 ## Check your learning

5.17 Is the following statement **True** or **False**?

> If you cannot go to a polling booth on the day of the General Election, you cannot vote.

🇬🇧 Standing for office

Most citizens of the UK, the Irish Republic or the Commonwealth aged 18 or over can stand for public office. There are some exceptions, including:

- members of the armed forces
- civil servants
- people found guilty of certain criminal offences.

Members of the House of Lords may not stand for election to the House of Commons but are eligible for all other public offices. 🇬🇧

Check your learning

5.18 Which two of the following can stand for election to Parliament?

☐ Members of the armed forces   ☐ Married women

☐ Members of the press   ☐ Civil servants

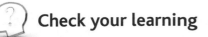 Visiting Parliament and the devolved administrations

The UK Parliament

The public can listen to debates in the Palace of Westminster from <u>public galleries</u> in both the House of Commons and the House of Lords.

You can write to your local MP in advance to ask for tickets or you can queue on the day at the public entrance. Entrance is free. Sometimes there are long queues for the House of Commons and people have to wait for at least one or two hours. It is usually easier to get into the House of Lords.

You can find further information on the UK Parliament website at www.parliament.uk.

Northern Ireland Assembly

In Northern Ireland elected members, known as MLAs, meet in the Northern Ireland Assembly at Stormont, in Belfast.

There are two ways to arrange a visit to Stormont. You can either contact the Education Service (details are on the Northern Ireland Assembly website at www.niassembly.gov.uk) or contact an MLA.

Scottish Parliament

In Scotland the elected members, called MSPs, meet in the Scottish Parliament building at Holyrood in Edinburgh (for more information, see www.scottishparliament.uk).

You can get information, book tickets or arrange tours through visitor services. You can write to them at the Scottish Parliament, Edinburgh, EH99 1SP, telephone 0131 348 5200 or email sp.bookings@scottish.parliament.uk

National Assembly for Wales

In Wales the elected members, known as AMs, meet in the Welsh Assembly in the Senedd in Cardiff Bay (for more information, see www.wales.gov.uk).

The Senedd is an open building. You can book guided tours or seats in the public galleries for the Welsh Assembly. To make a booking, contact the Assembly Booking Service on 0845 010 5500 or email assembly.bookings @wales.gsi.gov.uk

 Check your learning

5.19 Is the following statement **True** or **False**?

Any member of the public can visit Assembly or Parliament buildings and listen to debates.

Study tip

Explain what you have learnt to a friend and arrange to visit the nearest Parliament, Assembly or local council together. Compare the UK national and local governments with other countries you both know. What is the same or different?

Check your understanding

Now that you have finished Section 4 what do you remember about the following?

- Who can vote
- How you register to vote
- Where to vote
- Who can stand for public office
- How you can visit Parliament, the Northern Ireland Assembly, the Scottish Parliament and the Welsh Assembly

SECTION 5 The UK and international institutions

In this section you will read about the following:

■ **the Commonwealth and its role**

■ **the European Union and its role**

■ **other international institutions of which the UK is a member**

🇬🇧 The Commonwealth

The Commonwealth is an <u>association</u> of countries that support each other and work together towards shared goals in democracy and development. Most member states were once part of the British Empire, although a few countries that were not have also joined.

The Queen is the ceremonial head of the Commonwealth, which currently has 54 member states (see the table below). The Commonwealth has no power over its members, although it can suspend membership. The Commonwealth is based on the core values of democracy, good government and the rule of law.

Commonwealth members		
Antigua & Barbuda	Jamaica	Seychelles
Australia	Kenya	Sierra Leone
The Bahamas	Kiribati	Singapore
Bangladesh	Lesotho	Solomon Islands
Barbados	Malawi	South Africa
Belize	Malaysia	Sri Lanka
Botswana	Maldives	St Kitts and Nevis
Brunei Darussalam	Malta	St Lucia
Cameroon	Mauritius	St Vincent and the Grenadines
Canada	Mozambique	Swaziland
Cyprus	Namibia	Tanzania
Dominica	Nauru	Tonga
Fiji (currently suspended)	New Zealand	Trinidad and Tobago
The Gambia	Nigeria	Tuvalu
Ghana	Pakistan	Uganda
Grenada	Papua New Guinea	United Kingdom
Guyana	Rwanda	Vanuatu
India	Samoa	Zambia

Check your learning

5.20 Complete the following sentence:

The _____ is the ceremonial head of the Commonwealth, which currently has _____ member states.

The European Union

The European Union (EU), originally called the European Economic Community (EEC), was set up by six western European countries (Belgium, France, Germany, Italy, Luxembourg, and the Netherlands) who signed the Treaty of Rome on 25 March 1957. The UK originally decided not to join this group but it became a member in 1973.

There are now 27 EU member states (see below). Croatia will also become a member state in 2013.

EU member states		
Austria	Germany	Netherlands
Belgium	Greece	Poland
Bulgaria	Hungary	Portugal
Cyprus	Ireland	Romania
Czech Republic	Italy	Slovakia
Denmark	Latvia	Slovenia
Estonia	Lithuania	Spain
Finland	Luxembourg	Sweden
France	Malta	UK

EU law is legally binding in the UK and all other EU member states. European laws are called directives, regulations or framework decisions.

Check your learning

5.21 Is the following statement **True** or **False**?

In 1973 the UK joined the European Economic Community (EEC), which later became the European Union.

The Council of Europe

The Council of Europe is separate from the EU. It has 47 member countries, including the UK, and is responsible for the protection and promotion of human rights in those countries. It has no power to make laws but draws up conventions and charters, the most well-known of which is the European Convention on Human Rights and Fundamental Freedoms, usually called the European Convention on Human Rights.

The United Nations

The UK is part of the United Nations (UN), an international organisation with more than 190 countries as members.

The UN was set up after the Second World War and aims to prevent war and promote international peace and security. There are 15 members on the UN Security Council, which recommends action when there are international <u>crises</u> and threats to peace. The UK is one of five permanent members of the Security Council.

© ArtisticPhoto / Shutterstock.com

National flags

The North Atlantic Treaty Organisation (NATO)

The UK is also a member of NATO. NATO is a group of European and North American countries that have agreed to help each other if they come under attack. It also aims to maintain peace between all of its members.

Check your learning

5.22 Which of the following organisations drew up the European Convention on Human Rights?

☐ The North Atlantic Treaty Organisation (NATO)
☐ The Council of Europe
☐ The United Nations

Check your understanding

Now that you have finished Section 5, what do you remember about the following?

- What the Commonwealth is and what it does
- What the European Union is and its members
- Other international organisations of which the UK is a member

SECTION 6 Respecting the law

In this section you will read about the following:

■ **the law in the UK**

■ **the difference between civil and criminal law**

■ **the police and their duties**

■ **the possible terrorist threats facing the UK**

🇬🇧 One of the most important responsibilities of all residents in the UK is to know and obey the law. This section will tell you about the legal system in the UK and some of the laws that may affect you. Britain is proud of being a welcoming country, but all residents, regardless of their background, are expected to <u>comply</u> with the law and to understand that some things which may be allowed in other legal systems are not acceptable in the UK. Those who do not respect the law should not expect to be allowed to become permanent residents in the UK.

The law is relevant to all areas of life in the UK. You should make sure you are aware of the laws which affect your everyday life, including both your personal and business affairs.

The law in the UK

Every person in the UK receives equal treatment under the law. This means that the law applies in the same way to everyone, no matter who they are or where they are from.

Laws can be divided into criminal law and <u>civil law</u>:

■ Criminal law relates to crimes, which are usually investigated by the police or another authority such as a council, and which are punished by the courts.

■ Civil law is used to settle <u>disputes</u> between individuals and groups.

Examples of criminal law are:

■ Carrying a weapon: it is a criminal offence to carry a weapon of any kind even if it is for self-defence. This includes a gun, a knife or anything that is made or adapted to cause injury.

■ Drugs: selling or buying drugs such as heroin, cocaine, ecstasy and cannabis is illegal in the UK.

■ Racial crime: it is a criminal offence to cause <u>harassment</u>, <u>alarm</u> or distress to someone because of their religion or ethnic origin.

■ Selling tobacco: it is illegal to sell tobacco products (for example, cigarettes, cigars, roll-up tobacco) to anyone under the age of 18.

■ Smoking in public places: it is against the law to smoke tobacco products in nearly every enclosed public place in the UK. There are signs displayed to tell you where you cannot smoke.

■ Buying alcohol: it is a criminal offence to sell alcohol to anyone who is under 18 or buy alcohol for people who are under the age of 18. (There is one exception: people aged 16 or over can drink alcohol with a meal in a hotel or restaurant – see page 203.)

This list doesn't include all crimes. There are many that apply in most countries, such as murder, <u>theft</u> and <u>assault</u>. You can find out more about types of crime in the UK at www.gov.uk

Examples of civil laws are:

■ Housing law: this includes disputes between landlords and tenants over issues such as repairs and <u>eviction</u>.

■ Consumer rights: an example of this is a dispute about faulty goods or services.

■ Employment law: these cases include disputes over wages and cases of unfair dismissal or discrimination in the workplace.

■ Debt: people might be taken to court if they owe money to someone.

Check your learning

5.23 From the list below, decide which ones are criminal cases and which are civil cases, and put a tick (✓) under the right heading.

A case against:	Civil case	Criminal case
a landlord who refuses to do repairs		
a shop refusing to refund the cost of goods that do not work		
someone smoking on a train		
someone who owes you a lot of money		
a shop selling alcohol to people aged 16		
a woman refused promotion because of her ethnic origin		
a young person carrying a knife when he or she goes out in the evening		

Study tip

Some laws will be different from those of other countries, especially the ones to do with the age when young people are allowed to do certain things like smoke, drink, have sex or marry. It may help you to remember facts about UK laws by comparing them with other countries where you have lived; for example, how old you have to be before you can buy alcohol in another country.

⊞ The police and their duties

The job of the police in the UK is to:

■ protect life and property

■ prevent disturbances (also known as keeping the peace)

■ prevent and <u>detect crime</u>.

The police are organised into a number of separate police forces headed by Chief Constables. They are independent of the government.

In November 2012, the public elected Police and Crime Commissioners (PCCs) in England and Wales. These are directly elected individuals who are responsible for the delivery of an <u>efficient and effective</u> police force that reflects the needs of their local communities. PCCs set local police priorities and the local policing <u>budget</u>. They also appoint the local Chief Constable.

The police force is a public service that helps and protects everyone, no matter what their background or where they live. Police officers must themselves obey the law. They must not misuse their authority, make a false statement, be rude or abusive, or commit racial discrimination. If police officers are <u>corrupt</u> or <u>misuse their authority</u> they are severely punished.

Police officers are supported by police community support officers (PCSOs). PCSOs have different roles according to the area but usually patrol the streets, work with the public, and support police officers at crime scenes and major events.

All people in the UK are expected to help the police prevent and detect crimes whenever they can. If you are arrested and taken to a police station, a police officer will tell you the reason for your arrest and you will be able to seek legal advice.

If something goes wrong, the police complaints system tries to put it right. Anyone can make a complaint about the police by going to a police station or writing to the Chief Constable of the police force involved. Complaints can also be made to an independent body: the Independent Police Complaints Commission in England and Wales, the Police Complaints Commissioner for Scotland or the Police Ombudsman for Northern Ireland. 🇬🇧

Check your learning

5.24 Can you remember what the head of each police force is called?

🇬🇧 Terrorism and extremism

The UK faces a range of terrorist threats. The most serious of these is from Al Qa'ida, its affiliates and like-minded organisations. The UK also faces threats from other kinds of terrorism, such as Northern Ireland-related terrorism. All terrorist groups try to radicalise and recruit people to their cause. How, where and to what extent they try to do so will vary. Evidence shows that these groups attract very low levels of public support, but people who want to make their home in the UK should be aware of this threat. It is important that all citizens feel safe. This includes feeling safe from all kinds of extremism (vocal or active opposition to fundamental British values), including religious extremism and far-right extremism.

If you think someone is trying to persuade you to join an extremist or terrorist cause, you should notify your local police force. 🇬🇧

Check your learning

5.25 What should you do if someone is trying to persuade you to join a terrorist cause?

Check your understanding

Now that you have finished Section 6, what do you remember about the following?

- The difference between civil and criminal law
- The duties of the police
- Whom to contact if you have a complaint about the police
- Possible terrorist threats facing the UK

SECTION 7 The role of the courts

In this section you will read about the following:

- **the judiciary and its role**
- **the different criminal courts in the UK**
- **what to do to claim a small sum of money from someone else**
- **the role of solicitors**

The judiciary

Judges (who are together called 'the judiciary') are responsible for interpreting the law and ensuring that trials are conducted fairly. The government cannot interfere with this.

Sometimes the actions of the government are claimed to be illegal. If the judges agree, then the government must either change its policies or ask Parliament to change the law. If judges find that a public body is not respecting someone's legal rights, they can order that body to change its practices and/or pay compensation.

Judges also make decisions in disputes between members of the public or organisations. These might be about contracts, property or employment rights or after an accident.

Check your learning

5.26 Is the following statement **True** or **False**?

> If the judges decide that a government action is illegal they can tell the government to change its policies.

Criminal courts

There are some differences between the court systems in England and Wales, Scotland and Northern Ireland.

Magistrates' and Justice of the Peace Courts

In England, Wales and Northern Ireland, most minor criminal cases are dealt with in a Magistrates' Court. In Scotland, minor criminal offences go to a Justice of the Peace Court.

Magistrates and Justices of the Peace (JPs) are members of the local community. In England, Wales and Scotland they usually work unpaid and do not need legal qualifications. They receive training to do the job and are supported by a legal adviser. Magistrates decide the verdict in each case that comes before them and, if the person is found guilty, the sentence they are given. In Northern Ireland, cases are heard by a District Judge or Deputy District Judge, who is legally qualified and paid.

Crown Courts and Sheriff Courts

In England, Wales and Northern Ireland, serious offences are tried in front of a judge and a jury in a Crown Court. In Scotland, serious cases are heard in a Sheriff Court with either a sheriff or a sheriff with a jury. The most serious cases in Scotland, such as murder, are heard at a High Court with judge and jury. A jury is made up of members of the public chosen at random from the local electoral register (see pages 244-245). In England, Wales and Northern Ireland a jury has 12 members, and in Scotland a jury has 15 members. Everyone who is summoned to do jury service must do it unless they are not eligible (for example, because they have a criminal conviction) or they provide a good reason to be excused, such as ill health.

The jury has to listen to the evidence presented at the trial and then decide a verdict of 'guilty' or 'not guilty' based on what they have heard. In Scotland, a third verdict of 'not proven' is also possible. If the jury finds a defendant guilty, the judge decides on the penalty.

Youth Courts

In England, Wales and Northern Ireland, if an accused person is aged 10 to 17, the case is normally heard in a Youth Court in front of up to three specially trained magistrates or a District Judge. The most serious cases will go to the Crown Court. The parents or carers of the young person are expected to attend the hearing. Members of the public are not allowed in Youth Courts, and the name or photographs of the accused young person cannot be published in newspapers or used by the <u>media</u>.

In Scotland a system called the Children's Hearings System is used to deal with children and young people who have committed an offence.

Northern Ireland has a system of youth conferencing to consider how a child should be dealt with when they have committed an offence.

Check your learning

5.27 Which one of the following types of crime do the Magistrates' and Justice of the Peace Courts deal with?

☐   A   Minor criminal offences, such as driving over the speed limit
☐   B   Serious offences, such as murder

5.28 If an accused person is aged 10 to 17, where is the case dealt with in England, Wales and Northern Ireland?   _____

And in Scotland?   _____

Civil courts

County Courts

County Courts deal with a wide range of civil disputes. These include people trying to get money that is owed to them, cases involving personal injury, family matters, breaches of contract, and divorce. In Scotland, most of these matters are dealt with in the Sheriff Court. More serious civil cases – for example, when a large amount of compensation is being claimed – are dealt with in the High Court in England, Wales and Northern Ireland. In Scotland, they are dealt with in the Court of Session in Edinburgh.

The small claims procedure

The small claims procedure is an informal way of helping people to settle minor disputes without spending a lot of time and money using a lawyer. This procedure is used for claims of less than £5,000 in England and Wales and £3,000 in Scotland and Northern Ireland. The hearing is held in front of a judge in an ordinary room, and people from both sides of the dispute sit around a table. Small claims can also be issued online through Money Claims Online (www.moneyclaim.gov.uk).

You can get details about the small claims procedure from your local County Court or Sheriff Court. Details of your local court can be found as follows:

■ England and Wales: at www.gov.uk

■ Scotland: at www.scotscourts.gov.uk

■ Northern Ireland: at www.courtsni.gov.uk

Check your learning

5.29 Write down two types of case that are heard in County Courts, or Sheriff Courts in Scotland.

1._____   2. _____

🇬🇧 Legal advice

Solicitors

Solicitors are trained lawyers who give advice on legal matters, take action for their clients and represent their clients in court.

There are solicitors' offices throughout the UK. It is important to find out which aspects of law a solicitor specialises in and to check that they have the right experience to help you with your case. Many advertise in the local newspapers and in the *Yellow Pages*. The Citizens Advice Bureau (www.citizensadvice.org.uk) can give you names of local solicitors and which areas of law they specialise in. You can also get this information from the Law Society (www.lawsociety.org.uk) in England and Wales, the Law Society of Scotland (www.lawscot.org.uk) or the Law Society of Northern Ireland (www.lawsoc-ni.org.uk). Solicitors' charges are usually based on how much time they spend on a case. It is very important to find out at the start how much a case is likely to cost. 🇬🇧

🧠 Check your learning

5.30 Is the following statement **True** or **False**?

In England and Wales, if someone owes you less than £5,000 and is refusing to pay, you can use the small claims procedure to try to get your money back without using a lawyer.

5.31 Can you name two organisations that can help you find the right solicitor for your case?

1. _____

2. _____

Check your understanding

Now that you have finished Section 7, what do you remember about the following?

- The judiciary and its role
- The different criminal courts in the UK
- Youth courts
- What to do to claim a small sum of money from someone else
- What solicitors do and how to find one if you need to

SECTION 8 Fundamental principles

Britain has a long history of respecting an individual's rights and ensuring essential freedoms. These rights have their roots in the Magna Carta, the Habeas Corpus Act and the Bill of Rights of 1689 (see pages 47, 70 and 80), and they have developed over a period of time. British diplomats and lawyers had an important role in <u>drafting</u> the European Convention on Human Rights and Fundamental Freedoms. The UK was one of the first countries to sign the Convention in 1950.

Some of the principles included in the European Convention on Human Rights are:

- right to life
- <u>prohibition</u> of slavery and forced labour
- right to liberty and security
- right to a fair trial
- freedom of thought, conscience and religion
- freedom of expression (speech).

The Human Rights Act 1998 incorporated the European Convention on Human Rights into UK law. The government, public bodies and the courts must follow the principles of the Convention.

Check your learning

5.32 Which of the following statements is true?

> A The UK helped to decide the principles of the European Convention on Human Rights and was one of the first countries to sign it in 1950.
>
> B The UK agreed to the principles of the European Convention on Human Rights but only signed it in 1998.

⌗ Equal opportunities

UK laws ensure that people are not treated unfairly in any area of life or work because of their age, disability, sex, pregnancy and maternity, race, religion or belief, sexuality or <u>marital status</u>. If you face problems with discrimination, you can get more information from the Citizens Advice Bureau or from one of the following organisations:

- England and Wales: Equality and Human Rights Commission (www.equalityhumanrights.com)

- Scotland: Equality and Human Rights Commission in Scotland (www.equalityhumanrights.com/scotland/the-commission-in-scotland) and Scottish Human Rights Commission (www.scottishhumanrights.com)

- Northern Ireland: Equality Commission for Northern Ireland (www.equalityni.com)

- Northern Ireland Human Rights Commission (www.nihrc.com).

Domestic violence

In the UK, brutality and violence in the home is a serious crime. Anyone who is violent towards their partner – whether they are a man or a woman, married or living together – can be <u>prosecuted</u>. Any man who forces a woman to have sex, including a woman's husband, can be charged with rape.

It is important for anyone facing domestic violence to get help as soon as possible. A solicitor or the Citizens Advice Bureau can explain the available options. In some areas there are safe places to go and stay in, called refuges or shelters. There are emergency telephone numbers in the helpline section at the front of *Yellow Pages*, including, for women, the number of the nearest women's centre. You can also phone the 24-hour National Domestic Violence Freephone Helpline on 0808 2000 247 at any time, or the police can help you find a safe place to stay.

Female genital mutilation

Female genital mutilation (FGM), also known as cutting or female circumcision, is illegal in the UK. Practising FGM or taking a girl or woman abroad for FGM is a criminal offence.

Forced marriage

A marriage should be entered into with the full and free consent of both people involved. Arranged marriages, where both parties agree to the marriage, are acceptable in the UK.

Forced marriage is where one or both parties do not or cannot give their consent to enter into the partnership. Forcing another person to marry is a criminal offence.

Forced Marriage Protection Orders were introduced in 2008 for England, Wales and Northern Ireland under the Forced Marriage (Civil Protection) Act 2007. Court orders can be obtained to protect a person from being forced into a marriage, or to protect a person in a forced marriage. Similar Protection Orders were introduced in Scotland in November 2011.

A potential victim, or someone acting for them, can apply for an order. Anyone found to have breached an order can be jailed for up to two years for contempt of court.

Check your learning

5.33 If your husband, wife or partner is violent towards you, write down two things you can do to get help:

1. _____

2. _____

5.34 Is the following statement **True** or **False?**

Arranged marriages, where both parties agree to the marriage, are allowed in the UK.

Taxation

Income tax

People in the UK have to pay tax on their income, which includes:

- wages from paid employment
- profits from self-employment
- taxable benefits
- pensions
- income from property, savings and dividends.

Money raised from income tax pays for government services such as roads, education, police and the armed forces.

For most people, the right amount of income tax is automatically taken from their income from employment by their employer and paid directly to HM Revenue & Customs (HMRC), the government department that collects taxes. This system is called 'Pay As You Earn' (PAYE). If you are self-employed, you need to pay your own tax through a system called 'self-assessment', which includes a tax return. If HMRC sends you a tax return, it is important to complete and return the form as soon as you have all the necessary information.

You can find out more about income tax at www.hmrc.gov.uk/incometax You can get help and advice about taxes and completing tax forms from the HMRC self-assessment helpline, on 0845 300 0627, and the HMRC website at www.hmrc.gov.uk

Check your learning

5.35 Complete the following sentence:

People working for an employer have their tax taken automatically from their income through a system called:

☐ A Pay As You Earn (PAYE) ☐ B Self-assessment

National Insurance

Almost everybody in the UK who is in paid work, including self-employed people, must pay National Insurance Contributions. The money raised from National Insurance Contributions is used to pay for state benefits and services such as the state retirement pension and the National Health Service (NHS). Employees have their National Insurance Contributions deducted from their pay by their employer. People who are self-employed need to pay National Insurance Contributions themselves.

Anyone who does not pay enough National Insurance Contributions will not be able to receive certain contributory benefits such as Jobseeker's Allowance or a full state retirement pension. Some workers, such as part-time workers, may not qualify for statutory payments such as maternity pay if they do not earn enough.

Further guidance about National Insurance Contributions is available on HMRC's website at www.hmrc.gov.uk/ni

Getting a National Insurance number

A National Insurance number is a unique personal account number. It makes sure that the National Insurance Contributions and tax you pay are properly recorded against your name. All young people in the UK are sent a National Insurance number just before their 16th birthday.

A non-UK national living in the UK and looking for work, starting work or setting up as self-employed will need a National Insurance number. However, you can start work without one. If you have permission to work in the UK, you will need to telephone the Department for Work and Pensions (DWP) to arrange to get a National Insurance number. You may be required to attend an interview. The DWP will advise you of the appropriate application process and tell you what documents you will need to bring to an interview if one is necessary. You will usually need documents that prove your identity and that you have permission to work in the UK. A National Insurance number does not on its own prove to an employer that you have the right to work in the UK.

You can find out more information about how to apply for a National Insurance number at www.gov.uk 🏴

Check your learning

5.36 Is the following statement **True** or **False**?

A National Insurance number is all you need to prove that you have the right to work in the UK.

🏴 Driving

In the UK you must be at least 17 years old to drive a car or motor cycle and you must have a driving <u>licence</u> to drive on public roads. To get a UK driving licence you must pass a driving test, which tests both your knowledge and your practical skills. You need to be at least 16 years old to ride a moped, and there are other age requirements and special tests for driving large vehicles.

Drivers can use their driving licence until they are 70 years old. After that, the licence is valid for three years at a time.

In Northern Ireland, a newly qualified driver must display an 'R' plate (for restricted driver) for one year after passing the test.

If your driving licence is from a country in the European Union (EU), Iceland, Liechtenstein or Norway, you can drive in the UK for as long as your licence is valid. If you have a licence from any other country, you may use it in the UK for up to 12 months. To continue driving after that, you must get a UK full driving licence.

If you are resident in the UK, your car or motor cycle must be registered at the Driver and Vehicle Licensing Agency (DVLA). You must pay an annual road tax and display the tax disc, which shows that the tax has been paid, on the windscreen. You must also have <u>valid</u> motor insurance. It is a serious criminal offence to drive without insurance. If your vehicle is over three years old, you must take a Ministry of Transport (MOT) test every year. It is an offence not to have an MOT certificate if your vehicle is more than three years old. You can find out more about vehicle tax and MOT requirements from www.gov.uk

Check your learning

5.37 How old do you have to be to drive a car or motor cycle?

5.38 Is the following statement **True** or **False**?

Driving without insurance is a serious criminal offence.

Check your understanding

Now that you have finished Section 8, what do you remember about the following?

- The fundamental principles of UK law
- That domestic violence, Female Genital Mutilation and forced marriage are illegal
- The National Insurance and tax system

SECTION 9 Your role in the community

In this section you will read about the following:

■ **how to get more involved in the community where you live**

■ **values and responsibilities**

■ **being a good neighbour**

■ **getting involved in local activities and organisations**

■ **being a volunteer**

■ **looking after the environment**

🇬🇧 Becoming a British citizen or settling in the UK brings responsibilities but also opportunities. Everyone has the opportunity to participate in their community. This section looks at some of the responsibilities of being a citizen and gives information about how you can help to make your community a better place to live and work.

Values and responsibilities

Although Britain is one of the world's most diverse societies, there is a set of shared values and responsibilities that everyone can agree with. These values and responsibilities include:

■ to obey and respect the law

■ to be aware of the rights of others and respect those rights

■ to treat others with fairness

■ to behave responsibly

■ to help and protect your family

■ to treat everyone equally, regardless of sex, race, religion, age, disability, class or sexual orientation

- to work to provide for yourself and your family
- to help others
- to vote in local and national government elections.

Taking on these values and responsibilities will make it easier for you to become a full and active citizen.

Being a good neighbour

When you move into a new house or apartment, introduce yourself to the people who live near you. Getting to know your neighbours can help you become part of the community and make friends. Your neighbours are also a good source of help – for example, they may be willing to feed your pets if you are away, or offer advice on local shops and services.

You can help prevent any problems and conflicts with your neighbours by respecting their privacy and limiting how much noise you make. Also try and keep your garden tidy, and only put your <u>refuse bags</u> and bins on the street or in <u>communal areas</u> if they are due to be collected. 🏴

Check your learning

5.39 Which of the following might annoy your neighbours?

- ☐ A   Inviting them for a cup of tea or coffee
- ☐ B   Putting your rubbish bags on the street any time you feel like it
- ☐ C   Offering to help them carry heavy shopping
- ☐ D   Having noisy parties until late at night

🏴 Getting involved in local activities

Volunteering and helping your community are an important part of being a good citizen. They enable you to get to know other people. It helps to make your community a better place if residents support each other. It also helps you to fulfil your duties as a citizen, such as behaving responsibly and helping others.

How you can support your community

There are a number of ways in which you can support your community and be a good citizen.

Jury service

As well as getting the right to vote, people on the electoral register are randomly selected to serve on a jury. Anyone who is on the electoral register and is aged 18 to 70 can be asked to do this.

Helping in schools

If you have children, there are many ways in which you can help at their schools. Parents often help in classrooms, by supporting activities or listening to children read.

Many schools organise events to raise money for extra equipment or out-of-school activities. Activities might include book sales, toy sales or bringing food to sell. You might have good ideas of your own for raising money. Sometimes events are organised by parent–teacher associations (PTAs). Volunteering to help with their events or joining the association is a way of doing something good for the school and also making new friends in your local community. You can find out about these opportunities from notices in the school or notes your children bring home.

School governors and school boards

School governors, or members of the school board in Scotland, are people from the local community who wish to make a positive contribution to children's education. They must be aged 18 or over at the date of their election or appointment. There is no upper age limit.

Governors and school boards have an important part to play in raising school standards. They have three key roles:

- setting the <u>strategic direction</u> of the school
- ensuring <u>accountability</u>
- monitoring and evaluating school performance.

You can contact your local school to ask if they need a new governor or school board member. In England, you can also apply online at the School Governors' One-Stop Shop at www.sgoss.org.uk

In England, parents and other community groups can apply to open a free school in their local area. More information about this can be found on the Department for Education website at www.dfe.gov.uk 🇬🇧

Find out more

The government introduced 'free schools' in 2010. Parents and other organisations, such as religious groups, can apply for funding to set up a free school in their local area, which they control, rather than the local authority.

🇬🇧 Supporting political parties

Political parties welcome new members. Joining one is a way to demonstrate your support for certain views and to get involved in the democratic process.

Political parties are particularly busy at election times. Members work hard to persuade people to vote for candidates – for instance, by handing out leaflets in the street or by knocking on people's doors and asking for their support. This is called 'canvassing'. You don't have to tell a canvasser how you intend to vote if you don't want to.

British citizens can <u>stand for office</u> as a local councillor, a member of Parliament (or the devolved equivalents) or a member of the European

Parliament. This is an opportunity to become even more involved in the political life of the UK. You may also be able to stand for office if you are an Irish citizen, an eligible Commonwealth citizen or (except for standing to be an MP) a citizen of another EU country.

You can find out more about joining a political party from the individual party websites.

Helping with local services

There are opportunities to volunteer with a wide range of local service providers, including local hospitals and youth projects. Services often want to involve local people in decisions about the way in which they work. Universities, housing associations, museums and arts councils may advertise for people to serve as volunteers in their governing bodies.

You can volunteer with the police, and become a special constable or a lay (non-police) representative. You can also apply to become a magistrate. You will often find advertisements for vacancies in your local newspaper or on local radio. You can also find out more about these sorts of roles at www.gov.uk

Blood and organ donation

Donated blood is used by hospitals to help people with a wide range of injuries and illnesses. Giving blood only takes about an hour to do. You can register to give blood at:

- England and North Wales: www.blood.co.uk
- Rest of Wales: www.welsh-blood.org.uk
- Scotland: www.scotblood.co.uk
- Northern Ireland: www.nibts.org

Many people in the UK are waiting for organ transplants. If you register to be an organ donor, it can make it easier for your family to decide whether to donate your organs when you die. You can register to be an organ donor at www.organdonation.nhs.uk. Living people can also donate a kidney. 🏴

Find out more

Certain blood groups are more common amongst people from particular ethnic groups. For example, 25% of south Asian communities are blood group B. Rare blood group U negative is only found amongst people of African and Caribbean descent. It is important that people from all ethnic groups give blood.

🏴 Other ways to volunteer

Volunteering is working for good causes without payment. There are many benefits to volunteering, such as meeting new people and helping make your community a better place. Some volunteer activities will give you a chance to practise your English or develop work skills that will help you find a job or improve your curriculum vitae (CV). Many people volunteer simply because they want to help other people.

Activities you can do as a volunteer include:

- working with animals – for example, caring for animals at a local rescue shelter
- youth work – for example, volunteering at a youth group
- helping improve the environment – for example, participating in a litter pick-up in the local area
- working with the homeless in, for example, a homeless shelter
- mentoring – for example, supporting someone who has just come out of prison
- work in health and hospitals – for example, working on an information desk in a hospital
- helping older people at, for example, a residential care home.

There are thousands of active <u>charities</u> and voluntary organisations in the UK. They work to improve the lives of people, animals and the environment in many different ways. They range from the British branches of international organisations, such as the British Red Cross, to small local charities working in particular areas. They include charities working with older people (such as Age UK), with children (for example, the National Society for the Prevention of Cruelty to Children (NSPCC), and with the homeless (for example, Crisis and Shelter). There are also medical research charities (for example, Cancer Research UK), environmental charities (including the National Trust and Friends of the Earth) and charities working with animals (such as the People's Dispensary for Sick Animals (PDSA)).

© mangostock / Shutterstock.com

Volunteers are needed to help with their activities and to raise money. The charities often advertise in local newspapers, and most have websites that include information about their opportunities. You can also get information about volunteering for different organisations from www.do-it.org.uk

There are many opportunities for younger people to volunteer and receive <u>accreditation</u> which will help them develop their skills. These include the National Citizen Service programme, which gives 16- and 17-year-olds the opportunity to enjoy outdoor activities, develop their skills and take part in a community project. You can find out more about these opportunities as follows:

- National Citizen Service: at nationalcitizenservice.direct.gov.uk
- England: at www.inspired.com
- Wales: at www.gwirvol.org
- Scotland: at www.vds.org.uk
- Northern Ireland: at www.volunteernow.co.uk

Check your learning

5.40 Look at the list below. Can you write down one thing you can do as a volunteer for each type of organisation on the list:

1 Schools

_____

2 Political party

_____

3 Animal shelter

_____

4 Hospitals

_____

Looking after the environment

It is important to recycle as much of your waste as you can. Using recycled materials to make new products uses less energy and means that we do not need to extract more raw materials from the earth. It also means that less rubbish is created, so the amount being put into landfill is reduced.

You can learn more about recycling and its benefits at www.recylenow.com At this website you can also find out what you can recycle at home and in the local area if you live in England. This information is available for Wales at www.wasteawarenesswales.org.uk, for Scotland at www.recycleforscotland.com and for Northern Ireland from your local authority.

© FrameAngel / Shutterstock.com

A good way to support your local community is to shop for products locally where you can. This will help businesses and farmers in your area and in Britain. It will also reduce your carbon footprint, because the products you buy will not have had to travel as far.

Walking and using public transport to get around when you can is also a good way to protect the environment. It means that you create less pollution than when you use a car.

Check your learning

5.41 Complete the following sentence:

Shopping for products locally helps your _____, _____ and farmers in your area and in Britain.

Check your understanding

Now that you have finished Section 9, what do you remember about the following?

■ How to get more involved in the community where you live

■ Values and responsibilities

■ Being a good neighbour

■ Different ways you can help in local schools

■ The role of school governors and members of school boards and how you can become one

■ The role of members of political parties

■ Getting involved in local activities and organisations

■ The benefits of volunteering for yourself, charities and the community

■ The types of activities that volunteers do

■ How you can help look after the environment

Revision questions and end of chapter checklist

1   When was the voting age reduced to 18?

    Answer:

___

2   Who is the heir of Queen Elizabeth II?

    Answer:

___

3   What is the area each MP represents called?

    Answer:

___

4   In 1958 the Prime Minister was able to appoint a new group of people to the House of Lords. What are they called?

    Answer:

___

5   What does the Speaker of the House of Commons do?

    Answer:

___

6   What is a Secretary of State in the government?

    Answer:

___

7   What takes place every week in Parliament when the leader of the opposition can point out the government's weaknesses?

Answer:
_____

8   Are devolved administrations able to make laws about foreign affairs?

Answer:
_____

9   The Queen is the ceremonial head of an international organisation with 54 members. What is it called?

Answer:
_____

10 The UK is a permanent member of the Security Council of which international organisation?

Answer:
_____

11 If the police catch you drinking alcohol in an alcohol-free zone, will you have to go to a criminal or civil court?

Answer:
_____

12 Whom do the Police and Crime Commissioners in England and Wales appoint?

Answer:
_____

13 What are the lawyers who give advice on legal matters called?

Answer:

_____

14 What is the name of the European Convention that forbids torture, slavery and forced labour?

Answer:

_____

15 What is canvassing?

Answer:

_____

16 What kind of school can parents open in their local area?

Answer:

_____

17 Who can join the National Citizenship Service programme?

Answer:

_____

End of Chapter Five checklist

Now that you have come to the end of Chapter Five, tick the boxes when you have:

- read the study material

- made short notes, drawings and timelines to help you with your revision

- looked up words that you do not understand and made a note of them

- completed the 'Check your learning' and revision questions and checked your answers

- read the study material again for the questions you got wrong

Glossary

abolish	Put an end to an organisation officially.
accountability	Responsibility for what you do and the ability to explain your actions.
accreditation	Get a qualification or official document about your skills and experience.
administration	(here) The government and all the departments or ministries that carry out its policies.
adopt	To accept or start using something new.
affiliates	Other groups or individuals connected with an organisation.
alarm	To scare, frighten.
allegiance	Loyalty to something - for example, to a leader, a religion or a country.

allocate	To give an amount or share of something to a group or person.
amendments	Changes in the words in a document.
animal shelter	An organisation that looks after animals that have no homes.
arrested (police)	Taken by the police to a police station and made to stay there to answer questions about illegal actions or activities.
assault	The criminal act of using physical force against someone or attacking someone; for example, hitting someone hard.
budget	Money set aside for a particular project, to be used within a specified time.
charity	An organisation that raises money, usually to give help to those who need it or for a particular purpose; for example, for medical research, art or historic buildings.
chosen at random	Chosen by chance, without a plan or system.
chosen on merit	Chosen for their qualifications, skills and experience.
civil law	The legal system that deals with disputes between people or groups of people.
civil service	The departments within the government which manage the business of running the country (people who work for the government can be called civil servants).
coalition	A partnership between different political parties.
committee	A group of people who have been chosen for a particular function or to represent an organisation and make decisions for it.

communal areas	Areas shared by a group of tenants or neighbours.
comply	To follow a set of rules; for example, to obey the law.
constituency	A specific area where the voters who live in that place (its constituents) can elect an MP to represent them in Parliament.
contempt of court	Behaviour or action that is illegal because it does not obey the rules of a court of law.
continuity	With no changes for a long period of time.
contributory benefits	Money paid to you from a fund you have previously paid into.
convention (government)	An agreement about particular rules or codes of behaviour; for example, between countries, or the government and citizens of a country.
corrupt	Dishonest; for example, taking bribes or telling lies for gain.
coverage	The way newspapers, television and radio report events or subjects.
crises (crisis)	Situations or times that are extremely dangerous or difficult.
curriculum vitae (CV)	Written summary of qualifications, skills and work experience.
debate	To discuss or argue about a subject.
defendant	The person accused of a crime.
department	(here) Part of the government that deals with a particular area of work; a ministry.
detect crime	To find out the details about a crime.
devolution	The passing of power from central government to another group at a regional or local level, which is then called a devolved administration.

devolve	To pass power from one institution to another.
disputes	Disagreements that may have gone on for a long time.
drafting	Writing a document that will be changed later; for example, after discussing it with others.
efficient and effective	Working well and not wasting time; getting results.
electoral register	The official list of all the people in a country who are allowed to vote in elections.
eligible	Allowed by law.
entertain	To look after guests or visitors.
eviction	To legally force someone to leave the place they are living in.
extract	To take something out, especially using force.
far-right	Very right wing; for example, fascist groups.
first past the post	A system of election in which the candidate with the largest number of votes in a particular constituency wins a seat in Parliament.
fit for purpose	Good enough to do the job something is designed to do.
franchise	The right to vote.
functions	Duties or responsibilities.
gallery	A floor at a higher level that looks over a lower floor inside a large room or building.
harassment	To annoy, upset or be nasty to someone over a period of time.
heir to the throne	The person who will become king or queen after the present ruler.
impartiality	Not supporting one side more than others.
implement	To make a law, system or plan start to happen; to carry something out.

inherit	To get a position, money or property from someone else, usually after they have died.
institution	(here) A large official organisation with an important role in a country.
integrity	Ability to do what is morally right.
interpret the law	To explain or decide what the law means.
judge	The most important official in court; makes sure that what happens in court is fair and legal.
judiciary	All the judges in a country; together responsible for using the law of the land in the correct way.
jury (law)	People who are chosen to sit in court, listen to information about a crime and decide if someone is guilty or innocent.
keep in check	Control.
landfill	A place where rubbish or waste is buried in the ground.
legislate	Make laws.
licence	An official document that shows you are allowed to do or have something.
magistrate	A person who acts as a judge in a court case where the crime is not a serious one.
marital status	Information about whether a person is single, married, separated or divorced; often asked for on official forms.
media	All the organisations that give information to the public – newspapers, magazines, television, radio and the internet.
misuse their authority	Use power to get away with behaving badly or illegally.
nominate	To officially suggest someone for a job, position or prize.

objectivity	Based on facts and not influenced by personal beliefs or feelings.
opposition	In the House of Commons, the largest political party which is not part of the government is officially known as the opposition.
organ donor	Someone willing to give an organ (for example, heart, kidney or liver) to someone else, usually after death.
organ transplants	To remove an organ (for example, heart or kidney) or other body part from one person and put it into someone else's body.
overrule	When someone – or an organisation with more power – says no to a decision or suggestion from another organisation or person.
penalty (law)	Punishment for breaking the law.
photographic identification	An official document with a recent photograph of the named person on it.
policy	A set of ideas or a plan of what to do in a particular situation that has been agreed by a government, political party or organisation.
politically neutral	Not allowing political ideas to influence a person in a particular situation; for example, in a job.
prohibit/prohibition	To make something illegal.
proportion	The number or amount of one thing when compared with another.
proportional representation	An election system in which political parties are allowed a number of seats in Parliament that represents their share of the total number of votes cast.
prosecute	To accuse someone of a crime in a law court.
public appointments	Important jobs on government committees or in national organisations.

public body	A government department or a group of people who represent or work for the government and who work for the good of the general public.
public galleries	Seating on a higher floor from which the public can see and listen to debates in Parliament.
radicalise	Persuade others to accept extreme political views.
refuse bag	Bag for rubbish; bin bag.
rival viewpoints	Opinions held by different groups of people
rural	Countryside.
scrutinise	Examine all the details.
secret ballot	A written vote done in secret.
sentence	A punishment imposed by court.
shadow cabinet	Senior MPs of a political party not in government.
sheriff (law)	A judge in Scotland.
Speaker	The member of the House of Commons who controls how issues are debated in Parliament.
stability	When something is not likely to change or move.
stand for office	Apply to be elected; for example, as an MP or councillor.
statutory payments	Legally agreed payments.
strategic direction	A plan with goals to achieve.
summon	An official order to come to a place or do something.
suspend	To stop something from happening or working, usually for a short time.
The Phone Book	A book which contains names, addresses and phone numbers of organisations, businesses and individuals.
theft	The criminal act of stealing something from a

	person, building or place.
treaty	An official agreement between countries or governments.
valid	Current, has not run out.
Yellow Pages	A book that lists names, addresses and phone numbers of businesses, services and organisations in an area. Also available online at www.yell.com

Answers to 'Check your learning' questions

5.1 False

5.2 18

5.3 Any three of the following: the monarchy, Parliament, the Prime Minister, the judiciary, the police, the civil service, local government

5.4 B Queen Elizabeth II

5.5 ✓ A

5.6 MPs F
Leader of the Opposition E
Life Peers A
Speaker D
Prime Minister C
Members of the Cabinet B

5.7 B ✓ 5 years

5.8 False

5.9 A responsible for managing relationships with foreign countries
B responsible for the economy
C responsible for policing and immigration
D responsible for schools, colleges and universities

5.10

Political Party	Lobby Group
Conservatives	Liberty
Labour	CBI
Liberal Democrats	Greenpeace

5.11   A

5.12   Mayor

5.13   Members of the Legislative Assembly (MLAs)   **Northern Ireland**

       Assembly members (AMs)   **Wales**

5.14   Members of the Scottish Parliament (MSPs)

5.15   A

5.16   B

5.17   False

5.18   married women, members of the press

5.19   True

5.20   The <u>Queen</u> (or monarch) is the ceremonial head of the Commonwealth, which currently has <u>54</u> member states.

5.21   True

5.22   ✓ The Council of Europe

5.23

A case against:	Civil case	Criminal case
a landlord who refuses to do repairs	✓	
a shop refusing to refund the cost of goods that do not work	✓	
someone smoking on a train		✓
someone who owes you a lot of money	✓	
a shop selling alcohol to people aged 16		✓
a woman refused promotion because of her ethnic origin	✓	
a young person carrying a knife when he or she goes out in the evening		✓

5.24   Chief Constable

5.25   Tell the police

5.26   True

5.27   ✓ A Minor criminal offences, such as a driving over the speed limit

5.28   Youth Court

       Children's Hearings System

5.29   1 divorce   2 family matters

5.30   True

5.31 1 Citizens Advice Bureau 2 Law Society / of Scotland / of Northern Ireland

5.32 ✓ A

5.33 call / go to the police; call the National Domestic Violence Freephone Helpline; go to the Citizens Advice Bureau; or call the nearest women's centre

5.34 True

5.35 ✓ A

5.36 False

5.37 17

5.38 True

5.39 ✓ B

✓ D

5.40

1 Schools	help in classroom; join the PTA; fundraise; or become a school governor
2 Political party	canvass at an election; or stand for political office
3 Animal shelter	help care for animals; or fundraise
4 Hospitals	work on an information desk; give blood; or register as an organ donor

5.41 Shopping for products locally helps your <u>community</u>, <u>businesses</u> and farmers in your area and in Britain.

Answers to revision questions

1 1969
2 Prince Charles / Prince of Wales
3 Constituency
4 Life peers
5 Keeps order during political debates to make sure the rules are followed
6 Minister (in charge of a government department)
7 Prime Minister's Question Time

8   No
9   Commonwealth
10 United Nations (UN)
11 A criminal court
12 Chief Constables
13 Solicitors
14 European Convention on Human Rights
15 Persuading people to vote for a political candidate
16 Free school
17 16- and 17-year-olds

CHAPTER SIX

Taking the test

This chapter tells you how to book your test, what to expect on the day, what to take with you and what happens after you have taken the test.

It tells you more about preparing for the test. It also includes examples of the four types of question that are used in the test.

i NOTE

Remember, all the test questions will be about life in the UK, as described in the study material. Some questions will be about the part of the UK you live in – England, Scotland, Wales or Northern Ireland. Make sure that you pay special attention to that information.

This chapter is divided into four sections:

- ■ **Section 1** Booking your test
- ■ **Section 2** What to expect on the day of your test
- ■ **Section 3** Tips to help you when you take the test
- ■ **Section 4** What happens after the test?

SECTION 1 Booking your test

Can I take the test close to where I live?

You can take the test at one of the many test centres across the UK. When you book your test you are given the addresses of five centres near your home. You can choose the one that is most convenient for you.

Most test centres are also learning centres where you can improve your English language or computer skills.

How do I book my test?

Go to the site www.lifeintheuktest.gov.uk

You **must** register for an account on the site in order to take the test. To register for the test you need to have an email account. If you do not have an email address and do not have anyone to help you, go to your local library to find out where you can get help. (See below for further advice.)

You can also call the *Life in the UK* **test helpline** on **0800 015 4245** for advice and information.

i NOTE

This information is accurate for 2013 but the requirements and test fee could change in the future. Check the website www.lifeintheuktest.gov.uk for the most up-to-date information.

What information do I need to register?

When you register you have to provide your name, address and information on the photographic identification document (ID) you are using to prove that you are who you say you are. You will have to take this ID with you when you go to the test centre to take your test.

What forms of photographic ID can I use?

You must bring **one** of the following documents to the test centre with you (the document must include a photo that looks like you and must not be out of date):

■ **a biometric residence permit** – a residence permit containing your biometric information, facial image and fingerprints;

■ **a UK photocard driving licence**;

■ **a European Union identity card**; or

■ **an approved travel document** – for example, a UK Home Office travel document such as a convention travel document, a certificate of identity document or a stateless person document.

i NOTE

A **biometric residence permit** is a card that contains:

• your name, date and place of birth, and
• your 'biometric information' (fingerprints and facial image).

It also shows your immigration status and your entitlements while you are in the UK.

You can also use the following documents, which may be out of date (expired):

■ **a passport from your country of origin**; or

■ **an immigration status document**, endorsed with a UK residence permit with your photo.

If you do not have any of these documents you can contact the Home Office for advice.

Do I need to take any other documents with me when I go to the test centre?

In addition to a piece of photographic ID, you need to take an official document that has your name, address and postcode on it. It must be an original document, not a photocopy; for example:

- a gas/electricity/water bill
- a council tax bill
- a bank or credit card statement
- a UK photocard driving licence
- a letter from the Home Office with your name and address on it

You will not be able to take your test without one of the above documents, so please do not forget to bring it with you.

Can I choose a test session?

When you register online, you can choose a session at a time that suits you. The earliest you can take a test is seven days after you make your booking. So if you fill in the booking form on 1 June, the first date you can take the test would be 8 June.

What happens if I need to change the date of my test?

Tell your test centre as soon as possible. Your test fee will not be refunded if you cancel your test with less than seven days to go.

What happens if I have a disability and need special help to take the test?

You will be asked to let the centre know about particular needs when you book your test. This will give staff time to make any arrangements and provide the support you need. People with some disabilities do not have to take the test at all.

A special request includes:

- more time to take the test if you have a visual impairment (you cannot see very well);
- the help of a signer and more time to take the test if you've got a hearing impairment (you cannot hear very well);
- more time to take the test if you have a reading disability, such as dyslexia, or cannot read in your first language;
- the option to take your test in Welsh if the test centre is in Wales; and
- the option to take your test in Scottish Gaelic if the test centre is in Scotland.

The test is available in different formats or styles to meet particular needs, so you can choose to take your test in the format that suits you. Examples of these are on the *Life in the UK* test website www.lifeintheuktest.gov.uk

Is the test only available in English?

The test is in English. However, if you are taking the test in Scotland or Wales you can ask to take the test in Scottish Gaelic or in the Welsh language when you book your test.

How much will the test cost?

The test costs £50 in 2013. You need to pay this fee when you book your test by debit or credit card. If you do not have a credit or debit card, you can use a pre-paid credit card.

I have never used a computer. Can I take a written test?

No. You can only take the test using a computer at an official test centre. But you only need basic computer skills.

Practise using a keyboard and a mouse before you take the test. There are computer and keyboard practice exercises on the www.lifeintheuktest.gov.uk website.

There are lots of places where you can use computers, such as your local library. Some libraries offer training on how to use the internet. Many of the organisations where the test centres are based also offer training. They may be in learndirect or UK online centres, further education colleges, adult education centres or voluntary organisations. Training for people who are new to using computers is often free.

SECTION 2 What to expect on the day of your test

What will happen when I arrive at the test centre?

When you arrive at your test centre, the test supervisor will ask you to provide the ID you registered with and proof of your address. Without these documents, you will not be able to take your test and your test fee will not be refunded.

The test supervisor will check and record:

- your full name
- your date of birth
- your nationality
- your country and place of birth
- your postcode
- your Home Office reference number (if available)
- your purpose for taking the test
- that your photographic ID looks like you

He or she will tell you about the test conditions and will log you on to a computer.

Can I take anyone with me to the test centre?

You cannot take family members or friends into the test room with you and there may not be a waiting area for them.

Can I take a practice test at the centre?

You will have time to complete a practice test before you begin the *Life in the UK* test.

The test supervisor will tell you when to begin your test and how long you have to complete it.

Can I listen to the test questions?

When you take the test you can choose to listen to the questions. Ask for headphones.

If I live in Scotland, Wales or Northern Ireland, will there be test questions about those places?

The test questions will be about life in the UK, as described in the study material from the *Life in the United Kingdom: A Guide for New Residents* (3rd Edition) handbook (all the text is in this book in the passages marked with a Union Jack). The test will also include questions which ask you about the part of the UK that you live in – England, Scotland, Wales or Northern Ireland.

How long does the test last?

You will have 45 minutes to answer 24 questions. It is very important not to rush to finish the test. You should have enough time to choose your answers carefully and check them again before the end.

Does the test have a pass mark?

The pass mark is 75%. You have to get at least 18 answers correct.

Will I take the test by myself?

It depends where you are. There are usually about 15 other people taking the test at the same time.

Can I take books, notes or other equipment into the test with me?

No. You cannot take any books or notes with you and you are not allowed to use any electronic devices, such as a mobile phone.

What types of questions are there in the test?

There are four different types of multiple-choice questions. You choose the correct answer from one or more options. The following examples show you the different types of question. Remember that they are not real test questions.

Question type 1

The first type of question asks you to select **one** correct answer from four options.

What is the name of the admiral who died in a sea battle in 1805 and has a monument in Trafalgar Square, London?

○ Cook
○ Drake
● Nelson
○ Raleigh

The correct answer is **Nelson**.

In this question you need to choose one answer only. You click on the white circle next to your answer. When you click on the circle a black dot will appear in the centre to show you have selected it.

If you click on another circle and realise you have made a mistake, just click on the correct one to change your answer.

Question type 2

In this type of question you have to decide whether a question is **True** or **False**.

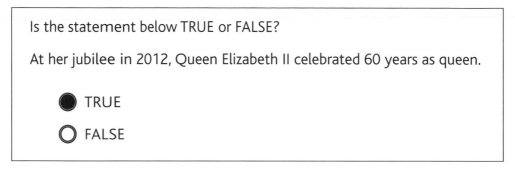

Is the statement below TRUE or FALSE?

At her jubilee in 2012, Queen Elizabeth II celebrated 60 years as queen.

⬤ TRUE

◯ FALSE

The statement is **TRUE**.

Question type 3

For the next type of question you need to select **two** correct answers from four options.

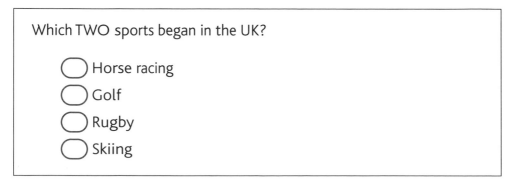

Which TWO sports began in the UK?

◯ Horse racing
◯ Golf
◯ Rugby
◯ Skiing

The correct answers are **Golf** and **Rugby**. When you click on one of the boxes a tick appears like this: ✔

Question type 4

For the last type of question you need to choose which one of two statements you think is correct.

Which of these statements is correct?

 ● The Prime Minister lives in Downing Street when in London
○ The Prime Minister lives in Chequers when in London

The correct answer is **The Prime Minister lives in Downing Street when in London**.

How do I know how much time I have left to complete the questions?

There is a **timer** on the computer screen that counts down the time from when you start the test and shows you how much time you have left.

Halfway through the test time, you will get a time alert. You will get two more time alerts at **ten** and **two** minutes before the end of the test.

What do I do if I want to change or check an answer to questions I did earlier?

There are boxes at the top of each question screen showing which questions you have answered and which you still need to answer.

At the bottom of the screen you can select **Previous question** to return to the previous question in the test. Selecting **Next question** takes you to the next question in the test.

Also at the bottom of the screen, **Questions left to answer** tells you how many questions you have left to answer. **Questions answered** tells you how many you have completed.

The **navigation tutoria**l on the site www.lifeintheuktest.gov.uk has examples of the test questions and shows you what you will see on the computer screen. Visit the site and get to know what the test looks like.

What happens if I run out of time?

The test will automatically end and you will not be able to click on any more answers on the screen. **However, most people finish with plenty of time**.

SECTION 3 Tips to help you when you take the test

Finally, the day of your test has arrived. Do you feel nervous? Are your hands sweating? Or are you calm and relaxed – even excited – that your journey to citizenship or settlement is nearly at an end?

If you have worked your way through this book and used the study tips that work best for you, you are well prepared – so be confident and believe in yourself. Remember that the questions are written to find out what you know, not to trick or confuse you.

The following tips will help you when you take the test. The most important thing is to stay as calm and relaxed as you can. Stress affects your concentration and can lead to mistakes.

Remember that, if you fail your test, you can take it again as many times as you need to.

Tips

- Make sure you get enough sleep before the day of your test. Your memory works better when you have had enough rest.

- Have something to eat and drink so that you are not hungry or thirsty. Take a snack and a bottle of water with you. Remember, your brain does not work so well when you have not had enough to drink.

- Plan your journey to the centre so that you arrive with plenty of time before the test and do not feel rushed.

- Remember to take the documents that you need to show the test supervisor. Check carefully that your personal details are entered correctly in the test system. It is your responsibility to make sure they are correct.

- Listen to the test supervisor's instructions carefully. Ask if there is anything you do not understand. The supervisor is there to help you.

Answering the questions

The test supervisor will offer you a practice test. Do it. This will give you the chance to practise using the computer and see what the test looks like on the computer screen. You will also be able to find out how it feels to answer the questions on the screen.

- Read the questions carefully to make sure that you understand them and know what to do.
- Remember that you can click on the **Hear the question** button any time you want to hear the question read out loud.
- Plan your time. Use the timer on the screen to help you.

> ### Did you know?
>
> Most people finish the test in about 22 minutes. You have 45 minutes, so do not rush.

Answer every question, even if you are not sure. There is a chance that you will choose the right answer. If there are only two possible answers, you have a 50/50 chance of getting the question right.

If you do not know the answer to a question with four choices, try to identify which options are obviously wrong. This will cut down the number of options to choose from.

Do not spend too much time on any one question – you can always go back to it later. Remember there are boxes at the top of the screen that tell you which questions you have answered, which you have just looked at, and which you have not seen yet.

If you find yourself getting so nervous that your mind goes blank, stop for a few moments. Take long, deep breaths and imagine a peaceful place. Remind yourself that you have studied hard and that you will not get into trouble if you do not pass.

SECTION 4 What happens after the test?

When do I find out the result of my test?

You get your result on the same day. The test supervisor will tell you whether you have passed the test while you are still at the centre.

I passed my test! What happens next?

Your test supervisor will give you a **pass notification letter** that you have to sign before you leave the test centre.

i NOTE

Your pass notification letter is very important. If you lose it, you cannot get another and you may have to pay to take the test again. Keep it in a safe place until you are ready to fill in your application for citizenship or indefinite leave to remain.

What happens if I fail the test?

You can take the test again but you will have to wait at least seven days to do so.

The notification letter will tell you which sections you got wrong and that you will have to study more carefully. If you got a lot of the questions wrong, you might want to spend more than seven days reading the study material and doing the practice tests in this book.

If I take the test again, will the questions be the same?

No. The computer chooses 24 questions at random from a selection of 400, so every test is different.

What should I do if the level of English was too difficult?

You should think about joining an adult ESOL class to improve your English. Some organisations offer ESOL with citizenship classes where you can improve your knowledge as well as your English. The test centre might have information about ESOL classes or you could ask at your local library, further education college or adult education centre.

CHAPTER SEVEN

Practice tests

Introduction

These practice tests are written in the same style as the *Life in the UK* test. Each one has 24 questions and includes all four types of the questions you will have to answer.

Wait until you have finished learning the study material and doing the ***Check your learning*** asks before you try any of these practice tests. This will give you a better idea of whether you are ready to book your test.

Time yourself and see if you can complete a test within 45 minutes (the time you are allowed when you take the official test).

If you get 18 questions or more correct, you have done very well – you are ready to take the *Life in the UK* test.

If you get between 15 and 17 questions correct, you have done well but you need to spend more time learning the study material and completing the ***Check your learning*** tasks. Use the study tips in Section 2 of Chapter One and elsewhere in the book.

If you get 13 or fewer questions correct, you really need to spend more time learning the study material and answering the ***Check your learning*** and revision questions before trying the practice tests again. If your test date is quite soon, it would be a good idea to change it to give yourself enough time to study.

Practice test 1

1 **Question** Elections in the UK have to be held at least every:
 Answer *(tick one box only)*

 A ☐ 4 years
 B ☐ 5 years
 C ☐ 6 years
 D ☐ 7 years

2 **Question** Which TWO of the following are banknotes in the UK?
 Answer *(tick two boxes only)*

 A ☐ £10
 B ☐ £25
 C ☐ £50
 D ☐ £100

3 **Question** What are members of the House of Lords called?
 Answer *(tick one box only)*

 A ☐ cabinet members
 B ☐ MEPs
 C ☐ Peers
 D ☐ Ministers

4 **Question** Is the following statement **True** or **False?**
 Answer *(tick one box only)*

 True ☐ The Queen is the head of state of all 54 countries in the Commonwealth.

 False ☐

5 **Question** What TWO things did Sake Dean Mahomet do for the first time in Britain?
 Answer *(tick two boxes only)*

 A ☐ Open a curry house
 B ☐ Introduce head massages
 C ☐ Sell tea
 D ☐ Smoke tobacco

6   **Question**   What was the name of the queen who fought against the Romans, whose statue is on Westminster Bridge in London?

Answer   *(tick one box only)*

A ☐ Anne
B ☐ Boudicca
C ☐ Claudia
D ☐ Victoria

7   **Question**   Which of the following statements is correct?
Answer   *(tick one box only)*

A ☐ The House of Commons checks laws that have been passed by the House of Lords.
B ☐ The House of Lords checks laws that have been passed by the House of Commons.

8   **Question**   Diwali is a festival in which religion?
Answer   *(tick one box only)*

A ☐ Buddhist
B ☐ Catholic
C ☐ Hindu
D ☐ Jewish

9   **Question**   Whom did the Jacobites support?
Answer   *(tick one box only)*

A ☐ Charles I
B ☐ Elizabeth I
C ☐ James II
D ☐ William III

10   **Question**   Which of the following was Oliver Cromwell's title as leader of the republic?
Answer   *(tick one box only)*

A ☐ King
B ☐ Lord Protector
C ☐ President
D ☐ Prime Minister

11	**Question**	In 2010 the population of the UK was just over:
	Answer	*(tick one box only)*

A	☐	50 million
B	☐	57 million
C	☐	60 million
D	☐	62 million

12	**Question**	What is the chairperson of the General Assembly of the Church of Scotland called?
	Answer	*(tick one box only)*

A	☐	Archbishop
B	☐	Elder
C	☐	Moderator
D	☐	Pope

13	**Question**	Is the following statement **True** or **False**?
	Answer	*(tick one box only)*

True	☐	Sir Isaac Newton discovered that white light was made up of all the colours of the rainbow.
False	☐	

14	**Question**	Which TWO of the following are shared goals of the Commonwealth?
	Answer	*(tick two boxes only)*

A	☐	Defence against the same enemy
B	☐	Democracy
C	☐	Development
D	☐	Free trade

15	**Question**	Which TWO of the following reforms did the Chartists campaign for in the 1830s and 1840s?
	Answer	*(tick two boxes only)*

A	☐	For MPs to be paid
B	☐	For separate governments for England, Scotland, Wales and Ireland
C	☐	For women to be allowed the vote
D	☐	Secret ballots

16	**Question**	Is the following statement **True** or **False**?
	Answer	*(tick one box only)*

True ☐   William, Duke of Normandy, was the last foreign invader to conquer England.

False ☐

17	**Question**	When was the National Assembly of Wales first formed?
	Answer	*(tick one box only)*

A ☐ 1997
B ☐ 1998
C ☐ 1999
D ☐ 2000

18	**Question**	Is the following statement **True** or **False**?
	Answer	*(tick one box only)*

True ☐   Inigo Jones designed the Queen's House in Greenwich in the 'gothic' style.

False ☐

19	**Question**	Is the following statement **True** or **False**?
	Answer	*(tick one box only)*

True ☐   British film makers have been famous for clever special effects since the 1890s.

False ☐

20	**Question**	Which of the following statements is correct?
	Answer	*(tick one box only)*

A ☐ The Church of Scotland is Presbyterian.
B ☐ The Church of Scotland is Catholic.

21	**Question**	Which TWO of the following are famous for their gardens?
	Answer	*(tick two boxes only)*

A ☐ Bodnant in Northern Ireland
B ☐ Sissinghurst in England
C ☐ Snowdonia in Wales
D ☐ The Trossachs in Scotland

22   **Question**   Which TWO of the following did the Labour government do to improve living conditions after 1945?

Answer   *(tick two boxes only)*

A   ☐   Created the National Health Service
B   ☐   Introduced annual elections
C   ☐   Nationalised the railways, gas, water and electricity
D   ☐   Introduced old age pensions

23   **Question**   Which of the following statements is correct?

Answer   *(tick one box only)*

A   ☐   King Charles I was crowned by Parliament in 1649.
B   ☐   King Charles I was executed by Parliament in 1649.

Question   Which of TWO the following are fundamental principles of British society?

Answer   *(tick two boxes only)*

A   ☐   Individual liberty
B   ☐   Republicanism
C   ☐   The rule of law
D   ☐   The right to bear arms

Answers to Practice test 1

1	B	9	C	17	C
2	A, C	10	B	18	False
3	C	11	D	19	True
4	False	12	C	20	A
5	A, B	13	True	21	A, B
6	B	14	B, C	22	A, C
7	B	15	A, D	23	B
8	C	16	True	24	A, C

Practice test 2

1 **Question** What are the plays with music and comedy that are performed at Christmas time called?

  Answer *(tick one box only)*

  A ☐ comic opera
  B ☐ murder-mystery
  C ☐ pantomime
  D ☐ tragedy

2 **Question** Which landmark is a prehistoric village built on Orkney, off the north coast of Scotland?

  Answer *(tick one box only)*

  A ☐ Newgrange
  B ☐ Offa's Dyke
  C ☐ Skara Brae
  D ☐ Stonehenge

3 **Question** Which of the following statements is correct?
  Answer *(tick one box only)*

  A ☐ The Speaker of the House of Commons is chosen by MPs in a secret ballot.
  B ☐ The Speaker of the House of Commons is chosen by the Prime Minister.

4 **Question** Which of the following statements is correct?
  Answer *(tick one box only)*

  A ☐ An allotment is a piece of land that people rent to grow flowers, fruit and vegetables.
  B ☐ An allotment is a piece of land that people rent to build a new home.

5 **Question** Which TWO of the following act as pressure or lobby groups?
  Answer *(tick two boxes only)*

  A ☐ Confederation of British Industry
  B ☐ Judiciary
  C ☐ Labour
  D ☐ Liberty

6   **Question**   Which of the following started the system of land ownership called feudalism?

Answer   *(tick one box only)*

A   ☐   Anglo-Saxons
B   ☐   Irish
C   ☐   Welsh
D   ☐   Normans

7   **Question**   Is the following statement **True** or **False**?
Answer   *(tick one box only)*

True   ☐   The Habeas Corpus Act guarantees that people arrested for a crime get a trial before being sent to prison.

False   ☐

8   **Question**   Who defeated the army of King Charles I and became the leader of the first republic in Britain?

Answer   *(tick one box only)*

A   ☐   Oliver Cromwell
B   ☐   Samuel Pepys
C   ☐   Henry Tudor
D   ☐   Sir Robert Walpole

9   **Question**   Is the statement below **True** or **False**?
Answer   *(tick one box only)*

True   ☐   Everyone living in the UK has the right to be treated equally by law.

False   ☐

10   **Question**   What percentage of the UK population lives in England?
Answer   *(tick one box only)*

A   ☐   67%
B   ☐   72%
C   ☐   84%
D   ☐   92%

11	**Question**	Is the following statement **True** or **False**?
	Answer	*(tick one box only)*

True ☐	At the start of the Industrial Revolution in the 18th century there were strict laws to protect workers.
False ☐	

12	**Question**	Which of the following is the festival that Muslims celebrate at the end of Ramadan?
	Answer	*(tick one box only)*

A	☐	Diwali
B	☐	Eid al-Fitr
C	☐	Hannukah
D	☐	Halloween

13	**Question**	Which TWO of the following problems did the government have to deal with in the 1970s?
	Answer	*(tick two boxes only)*

A	☐	Banking crisis
B	☐	Strikes by the unions
C	☐	War with Iraq
D	☐	Violence in Northern Ireland

14	**Question**	From what age can British people vote?
	Answer	*(tick one box only)*

A	☐	16
B	☐	18
C	☐	21
D	☐	25

15	**Question**	Anyone on the electoral register can be called to do WHAT in a court of law?
	Answer	*(tick one box only)*

A	☐	Act as a witness
B	☐	Become a magistrate
C	☐	Help the defendant
D	☐	Serve on a jury

16   **Question**   Is the following statement **True** or **False?**

          Answer   *(tick one box only)*

          True   ☐   The UK government has the right to suspend the Northern Ireland Assembly.

          False   ☐

17   **Question**   Which TWO of the following won gold medals for running?

          Answer   *(tick two boxes only)*

          A   ☐   Mo Farah
          B   ☐   Kelly Holmes
          C   ☐   Andy Murray
          D   ☐   Ellie Simmonds

18   **Question**   Which TWO of the following wrote poems about Scotland?

          Answer   *(tick two boxes only)*

          A   ☐   William Blake
          B   ☐   Robert Burns
          C   ☐   Walter Scott
          D   ☐   Dylan Thomas

19   **Question**   Which of the following statements is correct?

          Answer   *(tick one box only)*

          A   ☐   There are now more men than women in university.
          B   ☐   There are now more women than men in university.

20   **Question**   Which TWO of the following do civil servants do?

          Answer   *(tick two boxes only)*

          A   ☐   Carry out government policy
          B   ☐   Work for lobby groups that try to influence government policy
          C   ☐   Deliver public services
          D   ☐   Work for the opposition

21	Question	**Which of the following statements is correct?**
	Answer	*(tick one box only)*

A ☐ In 1688 **Protestants** in Parliament asked William of Orange to invade and proclaim himself king.

B ☐ In 1688 **Catholics** in Parliament asked William of Orange to invade and proclaim himself king.

22	Question	The Welsh National Assembly has the power to make laws for Wales in which TWO of the following areas?
	Answer	*(tick two boxes only)*

A ☐ Education
B ☐ Defence
C ☐ Housing
D ☐ Immigration

23	Question	**Which of the following statements is correct?**
	Answer	*(tick one box only)*

A ☐ Parliament gave women over the age of 21 the right to vote in 1870.

B ☐ Parliament gave women over the age of 21 the right to vote in 1928.

24	Question	Which of the following statements is correct?
	Answer	*(tick one box only)*

A ☐ You have to buy a TV licence for each television or other equipment that can be used to watch TV in your house.

B ☐ You only need one TV licence to cover the equipment in your home, except where you share a house with people with separate tenancy agreements.

Answers to Practice test 2

1	C	9	True	17	A, B		
2	C	10	C	18	B, C		
3	A	11	False	19	B		
4	A	12	B	20	A, C		
5	A, D	13	B, D	21	A		
6	D	14	B	22	A, C		
7	True	15	D	23	B		
8	A	16	True	24	B		

Practice test 3

1 **Question**   The Six Nations Championship is a famous competition for which of the following sports?
   Answer   *(tick one box only)*

   A ☐   Golf
   B ☐   Rugby
   C ☐   Skiing
   D ☐   Tennis

2 **Question**   Which of the following is a UNESCO World Heritage site?
   Answer   *(tick one box only)*

   A ☐   Hadrian's Wall
   B ☐   The Houses of Parliament
   C ☐   Edinburgh Castle
   D ☐   The Eden Project

3 **Question**   Which of the following statements is correct?
   Answer   *(tick one box only)*

   A ☐   A by-election is called when an MP dies or resigns in between general elections.
   B ☐   A by-election is called to choose a candidate for the General Election.

4 **Question**   Which of the following composers lived in the UK in the time of George I and II and became a British citizen?
   Answer   *(tick one box only)*

   A ☐   Britten
   B ☐   Elgar
   C ☐   Handel
   D ☐   Walton

5 **Question**   Is the following statement **True** or **False**?
   Answer   *(tick one box only)*

   True ☐   Sir Francis Drake was one of the the first to sail right around the world in his ship, the *Golden Hind*.

   False ☐

6 | **Question** | Which TWO of the following are Christian festivals?
| **Answer** | *(tick two boxes only)*

A ☐ Christmas
B ☐ Easter
C ☐ Eid al-Fitr
D ☐ Hannukah

7 | **Question** | Which TWO of the following does the Queen do as part of her official role?
| **Answer** | *(tick two boxes only)*

A ☐ Appoints the government after an election
B ☐ Chooses ministers
C ☐ Opens the new parliamentary session each year
D ☐ Tells the Prime Minister what laws to make

8 | **Question** | Is the following statement **True** or **False**?
| **Answer** | *(tick one box only)*

True ☐ The law says that when men and women do the same job, they should receive equal pay.

False ☐

9 | **Question** | How many houses or estates were there in the Scottish Parliament in the Middle Ages?
| **Answer** | *(tick one box only)*

A ☐ 1
B ☐ 2
C ☐ 3
D ☐ 4

10 | **Question** | What are shadow ministers?
| **Answer** | *(tick one box only)*

A ☐ Members of the cabinet
B ☐ Ministers' assistants
C ☐ Senior civil servants
D ☐ Senior opposition MPs

11	**Question**	Is the following statement **True** or **False**?
	Answer	(*tick one box only*)

	True ☐	April Fool's day is when lovers exchange cards and gifts.
	False ☐	

12	**Question**	What did the winner of the Nobel Prize for medicine, Alexander Fleming discover in 1928?
	Answer	(*tick one box only*)

	A ☐	Aspirin
	B ☐	DNA
	C ☐	Quinine
	D ☐	Penicillin

13	**Question**	Which of the following statements is correct?
	Answer	(*tick one box only*)

	A ☐	The BBC is the only wholly state-funded media organisation.
	B ☐	The BBC gets half its funding from advertisements and half from the state.

14	**Question**	Which TWO of the following groups of people were allowed to attend Parliament in the Middle Ages?
	Answer	(*tick two boxes only*)

	A ☐	Nobles
	B ☐	Women
	C ☐	Bishops
	D ☐	Serfs

15	**Question**	In what year did women get the right to vote at the age of 21?
	Answer	(*tick one box only*)

	A ☐	1918
	B ☐	1922
	C ☐	1928
	D ☐	1932

16 **Question** Which of the following statements is correct?
    Answer *(tick one box only)*

    A ☐ When Elizabeth I died in 1603 her cousin, James VI of Scotland, became king.
    B ☐ When Elizabeth I died in 1603 her cousin, William of Orange, became king.

17 **Question** Is the following statement **True** or **False**?
    Answer *(tick one box only)*

    True ☐ D-day was the day that atom bombs were dropped on Hiroshima and Nagasaki in the Second World War.

    False ☐

18 **Question** Which of the following is a group of European and North American countries that have agreed to help each other if they are attacked?
    Answer *(tick one box only)*

    A ☐ Commonwealth
    B ☐ European Union
    C ☐ North Atlantic Treaty Organisation
    D ☐ United Nations

19 **Question** Where is John O'Groats?
    Answer *(tick one box only)*

    A ☐ On the coast of Cornwall
    B ☐ On the east coast of England
    C ☐ On the north coast of Scotland
    D ☐ On the west coast of Wales

20 **Question** Is the following statement **True** or **False**?
    Answer *(tick one box only)*

    True ☐ The economy improved in the 1950s and working people had more money to spend.

    False ☐

21   **Question**   Which TWO of the following are part of Great Britain?

         Answer   *(tick two boxes only)*

         A   ☐   England

         B   ☐   Ireland

         C   ☐   The Isle of Man

         D   ☐   Wales

22   **Question**   Which of the following statements is correct?

         Answer   *(tick one box only)*

         A   ☐   Civil servants are appointed by political parties to support their policies.

         B   ☐   Civil servants are appointed on merit and have to be politically neutral.

23   **Question**   Which TWO of the following fought each other at the Battle of Waterloo in 1815?

         Answer   *(tick two boxes only)*

         A   ☐   Napoleon

         B   ☐   Nelson

         C   ☐   Washington

         D   ☐   Wellington

24   **Question**   Which of the following statements is correct?

         Answer   *(tick one box only)*

         A   ☐   The Opposition keeps order during political debates to make sure the rules are followed.

         B   ☐   The Speaker keeps order during political debates to make sure the rules are followed.

Answers to Practice test 3

1	**B**	9	**C**	17	**False**
2	**A**	10	**D**	18	**C**
3	**A**	11	**False**	19	**C**
4	**C**	12	**D**	20	**True**
5	**True**	13	**A**	21	**A, D**
6	**A, B**	14	**A, C**	22	**B**
7	**A, C**	15	**C**	23	**A, D**
8	**True**	16	**A**	24	**B**

Practice test 4

1   **Question**   Which of the following flowers is traditionally associated with Scotland?

        Answer   *(tick one box only)*

A	☐	daffodil
B	☐	rose
C	☐	shamrock
D	☐	thistle

2   **Question**   How much of the population did the Black Death kill in 1348?

        Answer   *(tick one box only)*

A	☐	a quarter
B	☐	a third
C	☐	half
D	☐	three-quarters

3   **Question**   Is the following statement **True** or **False?**

        Answer   *(tick one box only)*

True	☐	Adult citizens of other EU states who are resident in the UK can vote in all elections except General Elections.
False	☐	

4   **Question**   What is the name of the prize won by Sir William Golding, Seamus Heaney and Harold Pinter?

        Answer   *(tick one box only)*

A	☐	Man Booker
B	☐	Mercury
C	☐	Nobel
D	☐	Turner

5   **Question**   At what age can you apply for a free TV licence?

        Answer   *(tick one box only)*

A	☐	60
B	☐	65
C	☐	70
D	☐	75

6   **Question**   Which TWO of the following Roman forts can you see on
                          Hadrian's Wall today?
       Answer   *(tick two boxes only)*

       A   ☐   Caerleon
       B   ☐   Housesteads
       C   ☐   Cirencester
       D   ☐   Vindolanda

7   **Question**   Which of these statements is correct?
       Answer   *(tick one box only)*

       A   ☐   People in the UK have the right to freedom of belief and religion.
       B   ☐   People in the UK do not have the right to believe in some
                          religions.

8   **Question**   Which of the following ministers is responsible for crime, policing
                          and immigration?
       Answer   *(tick one box only)*

       A   ☐   Chancellor of the Exchequer
       B   ☐   Defence Secretary
       C   ☐   Foreign Secretary
       D   ☐   Home Secretary

9   **Question**   Which of the following statements is correct?
       Answer   *(tick one box only)*

       A   ☐   The devolved administrations in Northern Ireland, Scotland and
                          Wales each have their own civil service.
       B   ☐   The devolved administrations in Northern Ireland, Scotland and
                          Wales are run by the UK government's civil service.

10   **Question**   Which TWO of the following saints' days are celebrated in
                          March?
       Answer   *(tick two boxes only)*

       A   ☐   St Andrew
       B   ☐   St David
       C   ☐   St George
       D   ☐   St Patrick

11 **Question**   Who was the first Prime Minister of Great Britain?
   Answer   *(tick one box only)*

   A   ☐   Oliver Cromwell
   B   ☐   Winston Churchill
   C   ☐   William Pitt
   D   ☐   Sir Robert Walpole

12 **Question**   Who wrote the play *Hamlet* that has the line 'To be or not to be'?
   Answer   *(tick one box only)*

   A   ☐   Chaucer
   B   ☐   Dunbar
   C   ☐   Shakespeare
   D   ☐   Thomas

13 **Question**   Is the following statement **True** or **False?**
   Answer   *(tick one box only)*

   True   ☐   Causing distress to someone because of their race or religion is a
                 criminal offence.

   False   ☐

14 **Question**   Who was the Scotsman who invented the television in the
                   1920s?
   Answer   *(tick one box only)*

   A   ☐   John Logie Baird
   B   ☐   Tim Berners Lee
   C   ☐   Francis Crick
   D   ☐   Alan Turing

15 **Question**   Who was the first woman Prime Minister in the UK?
   Answer   *(tick one box only)*

   A   ☐   Harriet Harman
   B   ☐   Margaret Thatcher
   C   ☐   Theresa May
   D   ☐   Nicola Sturgeon

16   **Question**

Which TWO of the following are major stadiums where important sporting events take place?

Answer   *(tick two boxes only)*

A   ☐   Holyrood, Edinburgh
B   ☐   Millennium, Cardiff
C   ☐   Stormont, Belfast
D   ☐   Wembley, London

17   **Question**   Is the following statement **True** or **False**?

Answer   *(tick one box only)*

True   ☐

False   ☐   The Domesday Book tells the story of William the Conqueror.

18   **Question**   Is the following statement **True** or **False**?

Answer   *(tick one box only)*

True   ☐   The House of Commons is the more important of the two chambers in Parliament.

False   ☐

19   **Question**   Which TWO of the following hear minor criminal cases?

Answer   *(tick two boxes only)*

A   ☐   Chief constable
B   ☐   Justice of the Peace
C   ☐   Ombudsman
D   ☐   Magistrate

20   **Question**   Which of the following statements is correct?

Answer   *(tick one box only)*

A   ☐   Edwin Lutyens designed New Delhi to be the seat of government in India.

B   ☐   Edwin Lutyens designed the Tower of London to be the seat of government in the UK.

21   **Question**   Which TWO of the following are MPs' responsibilities?
             Answer   *(tick two boxes only)*

             A   ☐   To help to create new laws
             B   ☐   To nominate life peers
             C   ☐   To represent everyone in their constituency
             D   ☐   To select chief constables

22   **Question**   Is the following statement **True** or **False**?
             Answer   *(tick one box only)*

             True   ☐   In the 1960s the government encouraged people from the West Indies, India and Pakistan to settle in Britain.

             False   ☐

23   **Question**   From which TWO of these countries did Jewish people come to Britain to escape persecution in the 19th century?
             Answer   *(tick two boxes only)*

             A   ☐   Egypt
             B   ☐   Poland
             C   ☐   Russia
             D   ☐   Turkey

24   **Question**   Which of the following statements is correct?
             Answer   *(tick one box only)*

             A   ☐   Until 1870, when a woman got married, she kept her earnings, property and money.
             B   ☐   Until 1870, when a woman got married, her earnings, property and money belonged to her husband.

Answers to Practice test 4

1	D	9	A	17	False		
2	B	10	B, D	18	True		
3	True	11	D	19	B, D		
4	C	12	C	20	A		
5	D	13	True	21	A, C		
6	B, D	14	A	22	False		
7	A	15	B	23	B, C		
8	D	16	B, D	24	B		

CHAPTER EIGHT

Resources, references and useful websites

Life in the UK test website
This website contains up-to-date information about the test, including a sample test and help with using a computer keyboard and mouse. It is also where you book your test.

www.lifeintheuktest.gov.uk

Border Agency website

www.bia.homeoffice.gov.uk

Immigration enquiry bureau
This website has information about visas, immigration, British citizenship and studying and working in the UK.

www.ukba.homeoffice.gov.uk
ukbanationalityenquiries@ukba.gsi.gov.uk
0870 606 7766

Other government websites

GOV.UK
The official government website and the best place to find out about the government and all public services.

www.gov.uk

United Kingdom Parliament website
The official website for the UK Parliament, providing information about the House of Commons and the House of Lords, including the latest news about debates. It has an education page where you can learn more about the history of Parliament and how it works.

www.parliament.uk

Devolved administration websites

Northern Ireland   www.niassembly.gov.uk
Scotland   www.scotland.gov.uk
Wales   wales.gov.uk

Websites for further information and advice

Commonwealth website   **www.thecommonwealth.org**
Provides information about the work of the
Commonwealth and its member states.

European Union website   **www.europa.eu**
Provides information about the EU, its history, how it
works and its member states in many different
languages.

Citizens Advice websites   **www.citizensadvice.org.uk** and
An online advice service that provides independent   **www.adviceguide.org.uk**
advice on your rights, including benefits, housing,
employment rights and discrimination, debt and tax
issues.

Learndirect website   **www.learndirect.co.uk**
Learndirect freephone   0800 101 901
Learndirect Scotland   0808 100 9000
Provides online courses in basic English, Maths and IT as
well as other courses.

British Tourist Authority website   **www.visitbritain.com**
Provides information on places to visit such as historic
buildings, art galleries and museums, and places of
natural beauty as well as travel information.

Do it website   **www.do-it.org.uk**

Tells you all about volunteering and where you can get
involved in your local area.

School Governors' One-Stop Shop website   **www.sgoss.org.uk**

Provides information about becoming a school governor.
You can apply online to become a governor here.

Audio CD

Life in the United Kingdom: A Guide for New Residents
Audio CD (3rd edition 2013)
ISBN: 978 0 11341 360 7   Price: £12.99 (£15.59 inc. VAT)

Contains all the study material for you to listen to.